VOICES OF MICHIGAN STADIUM

*U of M Wolverine Football History told
by the Legends Who Made It*

JIM BRANDSTATTER

TABLE OF CONTENTS

PROLOGUE

University of Michigan Football has been around since 1879, and Michigan Stadium is coming up on its 100th birthday. And the football team is as popular as it has ever been! There is, without question, a history worth exploring in this institution we call Michigan Football. There have been millions of words written about this history. Stories and legends have been chronicled by hundreds who have attempted to put a face, a personality and an emotional component to the tradition of excellence Michigan Football has achieved. All of that work has added and strengthened the fabric of this incomparable program. But the foundation of this great success has always been about the people who built it--the people who nurtured it, the people who took it to new heights. We've read a lot about them. We have marveled at their commitment and their accomplishments. These people also had voices. And it is these voices and their contributions to Michigan's greatness that we celebrate in this project.

Voices like **Bo Schembechler***: If I ever let up my bitterness over what happened to that football team in 1973, I'm not being fair to those guys who played. So, I never have, and I've been bitter ever since about it, and I'll never forget it as long as I live.*

Or **Bob Chappius***: I had tears running down my cheeks, and I thought, gee whiz, I can't do this. And I looked at Bruce and there were tears running down his cheeks, too.*

Or Heisman winner **Desmond Howard***: I don't even think Mo seen it when it first happened, I really don't. He was just so happy that, you know, I scored and everything. I don't think he really saw. He probably didn't know until afterwards that I did the pose.*

Or the guy who scored the first touchdown ever at Michigan Stadium, **Kip Taylor***: I was at the right end and Oosterbaan was at the left. And they were trying to hit Oosterbaan with all the passes. Normally, naturally, that's right, because he was a great receiver--one of the finest athletes I've ever known and a great friend.*

Or **Ron Johnson:** *One of the statisticians came down and said, 'Ron, how many yards do you think you have?' And I said, "Probably 200." He said, "You got 347 yards," And I mean, my mouth just dropped.*

These are just a few short portions of the stories we've gathered. There are plenty more. Some you may remember. Some you may have never heard. Some may surprise you. Some may make you smile. And some may bring a tear to your eye. It's all part of the history of this great program. It's all in the Voices of Michigan Stadium.

PART ONE

BACK IN THE DAY

Michigan Stadium has seen a lot of firsts, but there will never be another first like Kip Taylor's. You see, back in 1927, in the first game ever played at the Big House; Kip Taylor scored the first ever touchdown at this iconic venue. It was against Ohio Wesleyan during a Wolverine, 33 to nothing victory. It was the only game Taylor started that season. As a matter of fact, Kip only played in three games for Michigan. You see, in his third game he suffered a career ending neck injury. Kip Taylor was born in 1909 and passed away at the age of 94.

Before he passed, I got a chance to meet Mr. Taylor at a function hosted by then-athletic director Don Canham in the early 2000's. Kip was full of vim and vigor and his mind was as sharp as a tack. It was a perfect opportunity to get the story of the first touchdown ever at Michigan Stadium directly from the man who scored it. A wonderful guy with a salty sense of humor and similar vocabulary, Kip's memory of that historic touchdown was as clear as it could be.

Kip Taylor: *In 1927, I had entered the university in 1926 and was a freshman there with Bill Orwig, and we had a lot of a lot of good kids, all freshmen. So, I went out for football and hell they said, "Well, you haven't got enough speed for halfback." I said, "Okay." So, they said, "We're going to move you to an end." I didn't know anything about end play, and so they moved me there.*

So, God, pretty soon I'm up on the number one team. My dad would say, "Son, how are you coming?" "Well, Dad, all right, I guess. I'm on the number one team." "What?" he said, and that's it. "When's the first game?" So, Dad went back and bought tickets.

So, we played the opening game and I was at right end, and Oosterbaan was at the left. They were trying to hit Oosterbaan with all the passes. Normally, naturally, that's right because he was a great receiver--one of the finest athletes I've ever known, and a great friend.

So, after getting down there and running until my tongue was hanging out, I came back and I say, "Throw that God damned ball to me, I'm wide open...shut up you sophomore." About three plays later, Louie Gilbert, who was an All-American halfback playing left halfback, called the same damn pass play. The right end was to run diagonally, and the left end come down and cut right by him, and as he cut, he was to hit him. Well, I thought, well, I can carry out my assignment. So, in we go, and the play ball is snapped back. I run down there and I thought, well, all I got to do is try and keep this man from getting it, and I looked up and there's the God dammed ball. So, I caught it. I had played a halfback in high school and I said, I guess I better run towards the goal. So, I went down, stiff-armed one, side-stepped the other and went in to score. No idea it was number one. My dad was in the bleachers, and I think I can still hear him yelling, because he had been a Canadian hockey player and he loved athletics and when I was an athlete, he was the proudest guy in the world.

With this amazing witness and participant in Michigan football history sitting right in front of me, I kept telling myself, don't let this opportunity get away. Kip Taylor was a treasure trove of tales from the very beginnings of the Michigan Football legend. As he was telling me his touchdown story, my mind flashed to the years he was talking about. It was the 1920's. I wondered, did Kip have any Fielding Yost memories? Yost is, of course, one of the most iconic names in Michigan Athletics history. His vision to build Michigan Stadium to the scale he built it, is why this book is being produced. To have someone who knew Yost firsthand, and maybe had interacted with a great man was an opportunity I could not pass up. So, as Kip regaled me with his Michigan memories, I asked him, "Did you get a chance to meet Coach Yost?" Taylor's answered did not disappoint.

> **Kip Taylor**: *Yost had coached up until the year before. But he came down on the field and, you know, he was a great teacher. I'll give you a little example: This is a goal line. The old man got us all around there, and he said, "Do you know what that is?" And we said, "Yes, that's the goal line." So, he stepped over, he stepped back, he stepped over, and he stepped back--I bet he did that twenty times. We all said, "Geez, this guy's off his rocker." He says, "Don't you know I can do this all day and all night, and it won't count a damn thing if I hadn't got that little brown thing under my arm." And you never forgot it. That was his way of telling you hang on to the damn ball if you're going over that goal line, because it isn't going to count if you haven't got it. Never forgot it!*
>
> *And other little things that he would do. Like, I know that he was the only coach I know of that could coach two major football teams the same year and win championships in both. Fielding H. Yost at Michigan and Fielding H. Yost was writing all of the plays, all of the practices, out to the Pacific Coast Conference to Stanford, and both of them won championships in the same year…I don't know how many people know about it, but that's the God's fact.*

While Taylor might have thought Yost was off his rocker at times, history has proven Yost was anything but off his rocker. In truth, Yost was a visionary. He created a physical plant for athletics that was second to none. His commitment to building facilities designated specifically for women is another part of his legacy that doesn't get mentioned enough. And this ambitious agenda was spelled out by Yost in the early 1920's, when his vision wasn't exactly embraced by some others. But he delivered, and his promise of athletics for all is very much alive to this very day at the University of Michigan. If you don't believe me, listen to the great Forest Evashevski, another legendary figure in Michigan athletic history.

After he graduated from U of M with his teammate and friend Tom Harmon, Evy went on to coaching greatness at Iowa. He also served as the Hawkeyes' athletic director during a glorious period in Iowa athletics. But, when it came to Yost, Evashevski was lavish in his praise.

> **Forest Evashevski:** *I think over the years, I think the aura that surrounded Michigan Stadium was brought by Fielding Yost, who was quite a man, did an awful lot for Michigan. And if you think of the foresight that man had, not only with a football stadium, but the ice rink, the intramural building and a golf course--he had the greatest physical plant for students of anybody I know. I knew him very well. In fact, he invited Tom and myself over for dinner after our sophomore year. He was talking, he said, "Don't you know, we graduate together." I didn't know exactly what he meant, but then I figured it out; when we graduated, he retired.*

Clearly, the Yost impact on Michigan is massive. As a football coach, he is unmatched. As athletic director, he's also legendary. And while his vision and completion of the physical plant in Ann Arbor is an incredible accomplishment, remember, he was also in charge of athletic personnel. Yost had to bring in the right people to shepherd the athletic programs forward. The excellence that he started had to have the right leadership and Yost delivered in that area as well.

For instance, in 1929, Yost dismissed Tad Weiman as Michigan's football coach and he hired a former player of his to take over. That player was Harry Kipke. As a player in the early 20's, Kipke was considered one of the best players in the country. The finest punter in the nation, he was also an excellent ball carrier, passer, and blocker. During his three varsity seasons with Yost as his coach, Kipke and Michigan won 19 games, lost only one, and tied two. In his first season as coach. He was only five, three, and one. But, in his second year, 1930, Kipke led his team to an unbeaten season and a Big 10 title. He was a fabulous recruiter and he led the program into the next era of excellence when Fritz Crisler would take over.

But it was Kipke's loyalty to Michigan and a little-known story that gives him legendary status in the history books of Wolverine football. At the end of Kipke's coaching tenure, the team had been struggling and Kipke was replaced. It was a controversial decision at the time, but it made way for Fritz Crisler to come on board. The little-known story about Kipke's departure was told to me by a gentleman named Howard Wikel.

Howard was a lifelong Ann Arbor resident. He played football at Michigan in 1943, and was the baseball team's starting shortstop and captain as a student athlete. But more importantly was Howard's life after he graduated from Michigan. He became an Ann Arbor community leader; he was an institution around town and stayed very close to the athletic department--so close, you'd have thought he was on the staff! He became great friends with the athletes and coaches throughout seven decades and in later life, Bo Schembechler considered Howard one of his closest friends. Athletes and players confided in Howard over the years and he was an encyclopedia of information on the inner workings of Michigan's athletic machine. He was also a great friend, and one of the most wonderful gentlemen I've ever had the pleasure to know. It was during a conversation with Howard when he told me this tale about the great Harry Kipke. The events in this story had major ramifications on the career of Fritz Crisler. And yet, it was all on account of the class and loyalty of one Harry Kipke.

Howard Wikel: *Kip had great teams in the early 30's--I think '32, '33, '34, and then he ran on bad times '35, '36, '37 and he was replaced. '38 or '39 was Fritz's first year. Now, Kipke had recruited Harmon, Kromer, Evashevski, Westfall, Ingalls, etc., and he was let go. And I would say every one of those players to a man, went to Kipke and said, "Do you want me to stay at Michigan?"...Everyone, to the man, said, "We're going to leave because they had let Kipke go." And he said, "No, you definitely stay here and play for Michigan." So, Fritz was handed almost an All-World team. The following year, had he stayed--of course, you never know what would have happened—but with what he had* *coming in, the chances are pretty good he was going to win a lot of football games, you know. He had everyone you could think of, so there were some hard feelings around but not outwardly from Kip...He was a class act. He chewed tobacco, but he was he was really a good guy.*

Following nice-guy Kipke into the head coaching position at Michigan is another iconic name in Wolverine history: Herbert Orin Fritz Crisler. Fritz came to Michigan with a sparkling resume having coached at University of Chicago, Minnesota, and Princeton. At Princeton, he won a couple of national championships. He added another national title at Michigan in 1947. Hired by Yost with a background that included working under the legendary Amos Alonzo Stagg, Fritz Crisler was a no-nonsense coach. He demanded respect from his players and at times, unlike Harry Kipke, Crisler may not have been the nicest guy on the outside. Fritz was determined to get results--good results. Michigan great Don Lund, who was a nine-time varsity letter winner at Michigan and who played for Crisler, remembers a practice when the toughness of Crisler was on full display. But it was a toughness wrapped around a lesson.

Don Lund*: This is back in '42. Now, we're gonna play Great Lakes, and Great Lakes has all these All-Americans and ex-pros, and that's our opening game. Our last scrimmage out here on Ferry Field, Tom Kuzma, our key halfback is running with the ball and cuts through, and a guy named George Kiesel hit him and he twisted his knee. So, he's in pain and Ray Roberts, his trainer, is over there and Fritz walks over, looks, and he said, "Move the team or move the body." As you look at that, in later years, you say, well, what he didn't want us to do is get down in the dumps. And Bob Chappuis was a sophomore then--we were sophomores together--and when Chapp played in the game, he looked like he'd been playing all his life. He stood back and threw the passes and did all the things, and we beat them nine to zip. So that was the basic idea. I mean, Fritz's, he was tough. He'd just look at you, he had that that mystique if that's the word, he just looked and you'd say, "Geez, what'd I do wrong?"*

Now, if you're thinking: *Come on, coaches didn't do that stuff, did they?* Well, there are different ways to motivate players, and there are different ways to make your point to the other players. Fritz Crisler clearly had a way about him that got the best out of his charges. To illustrate that, coach Crisler was consistent in his methods. Listen to Al "The Ox" Wistert. Al is one of the three Wistert brothers who played football at Michigan. The other two were Whitey and Alvin. All of them wore the number 10 and all of them were All-American tackles, and their number 10 is now one of the few retired numbers at Michigan. Legendary players all, but as good as they were, they got the same treatment from Coach Crisler in this tale from Al "The Ox" Wistert.

> **Al Wistert**: *My sophomore year, I broke an ankle. Fritz always said, put ankle wraps on to protect your ankles. And this day, I got to practice late, didn't put ankle wraps on, and I went out there in a scrimmage and broke an ankle. And as the trainer takes my shoe off, and then my sock, trying not to kill me, you know, because the ankle is broken, Fritz is standing there, and he sees no ankle wrap--bare skin. And he says, "Where's your ankle wrap, Wistert?" And I said, "I was late getting the practice, Coach, and I didn't put it on." He says, "Well, serves you're right." He says, "Well, move the ball or move the body. Let's not waste any more time here."*

Crisler clearly had a way of admonishing his troops without taking them apart. Here's another tale from the legendary Bob Chappius, who we will hear from later about Coach Crisler's methods in keeping his players solidly grounded.

> **Bob Chappius**: *And Jim Brieske, who was another sophomore, kicked a field goal—he missed the point but kicked the field goal--and we beat them nine to nothing. He came from a little town in Michigan called Harbor Springs. Well, anyway, Jim was so elated; he had never been in a game before for Michigan and would not get into too many more after that, except to kick field goals. But anyway, he came into the locker room*

after that game, and he had a newspaper. I don't know whether it was from Harbor Springs--the Harbor Springs Chronicle or whatever it was--and he had a headline, and it said, 'Jim Brieske: the Pride of Harbor Beach.' Big headline, and he brought it into the locker room, showed it to us. And then from there, from our locker room, he went into the coach's room and showed it to the coaches, which was a bad mistake.

Anyway, we got out to practice and Crisler put him on defense. And he was on his back all day. They were just knocking him down, and he was he was a linebacker, and not a very good one. He was on his back time after time. And finally, he was laying there, and Fritz went up, went over and looked down at him and he said, "Brieske, you're not the 'Pride of Harbor Beach.' You're a jackass." You know that of course, you heard that many times. That was the only, the only thing that Fritz ever would say of any nature. He wouldn't ever swear or do anything like that…Yeah, and if you were real bad, you were a double jackass.

While some of you may think it kind of hard on these young men to seem that cold, none of these players indicated to me that they remembered Fritz being mean or a tyrant. They instead remembered him and smiled. They spoke about him with great reverence. The gentleman who I spoke with that played for Coach Crisler, to a man, had nothing but the highest respect for him. They all figured out later in life that Crisler was about making them better, and they appreciated him for that effort.

One of these young men was Bob Chappius, who you just heard from a moment ago. Chappius was as good as they got as a football player. He was the linchpin of the Crisler's mad magicians of 1947, who won the National Championship. An All-American, Rose Bowl MVP, and runner up for the Heisman trophy, Chappius missed some of his college years because of his military service. He flew aboard a B-25 bomber in missions over Europe during World War II. His plane was shot down in 1945, and he spent three months hiding from the Germans behind enemy lines thanks to the Italian resistance. It was after these harrowing experiences that Bob returned to Ann Arbor and Michigan to complete his football career under Crisler. It is in that context that this war hero explains the impact a man like Crisler had on him.

Bob Chappuis: *He had the respect of all of us so much. His favorite term was, "You got to play better than you know how." You know, that was his approach. And by golly, we did that. Because as I've said many times, we didn't have great football players; we had good football players, and we all knew one another and respected one another and this may sound like an old cliché, but we did have the chemistry. And we knew what everybody else was doing and so forth. I suppose maybe Bump Elliot was the best player we had. But, beyond that--and I don't mean this unkindly to anybody because, you know, we had a good football team. We had to have, because we were undefeated; we went to the Rose Bowl and won that game rather handily. We went out there, you know, and we took the train. It took us about, I think, three days to get there on the train with a stop in Colorado. When we got out there, we checked in at the practice field, and we had a several two-a-day practices because we went out there three weeks ahead of time.*

Two days before the game, we were just running through plays at the end of practice to kind of work up a sweat and then go in. I was running this one play, and I went down and I had a terrible pain in my leg. And I didn't know exactly what had happened, but I had an idea that I had pulled a hamstring. I was on the ground and I was really in pain. Fritz came over—you know, I have a tough time calling him Fritz. It was always Coach or Mr. Crisler, most of the time it was Coach, but never Fritz. So, if I stutter a little bit on that word—anyway, he came over and he looked down at me. And then he looked at Jim Hunt, the trainer, and he said, "Jim, what happened here?" Jim said, "Well, I think Bob has pulled a hamstring." Coach looked down at me and he said, "Good thing it didn't happen to somebody that could run." I'll tell you, I never got up off the ground so fast in all my life. I mean, I just thought, "Well, gee whiz, I didn't think I'd been that bad that year.

Anyway, many, many years later, I was talking with some of the guys up in Ann Arbor and we were talking about that. Bruce Hilkene said, "Well you know, the players were kind of shook up about this." But he said, "When Fritz looked down at you—when Mr. Crisler looked down at you—what he said made us feel a lot better. We knew we could get along without you." You know, and that's, of course, exactly what he wanted! Number one, he wanted me to get off the ground, and number two, he wanted the players to know that I wasn't the only guy there. I mean, he was so great at that, with the way he said things, and they were all very sort of a monotone and you know, and very serious. And you knew when he said something, he really knew what he was talking about.

They put some tape on my on my leg, and at halftime I had them take it off because I was running slower than usual. So anyway, that was a great game. Of course, after the undefeated season, we beat Southern California forty-nine to nothing. It was really quite a climax.

It's pretty clear coach Crisler never missed a trick. A motivator, a leader, and maybe most impressive, an innovator. Remember, it was Fritz who put Michigan football players in the winged helmet to help in the forward passing game. He was the inventor of two platoon football. He was a genius at the X's and O's. He had the respect of his players in the college football community nationwide. And during his time as coach and then athletic director, Crisler oversaw 19 national titles, and an astounding seventy-four Big 10 titles. But deep down, Fritz was always a coach. He knew how to motivate and get the best out of his players, especially for a rivalry game like Michigan State. Al Wistert remembers one pregame talk before Crisler and his Wolverines met MSU.

Al Wistert*: Oh, yeah, I can remember one pep talk that he gave for us against Michigan State. He said, "You know, Michigan State—" and he said this as though he was turning up his nose, you know. Michigan State, he says, "Now, they never heard of Michigan State until they beat us." He said, "You guys made them, now I want you to go out there today and break them."*

During his tenure as coach at Michigan, there's only one guy that Crisler didn't have to push or motivate to get his best; that guy was Tom Harmon. He wore number 98, and that number is rightfully retired at Michigan. In 1940, Harman became the first Michigan player to win the Heisman trophy. He won the Maxwell award, symbolic of the best player in the nation. He was named the Male Athlete of the Year, he was a unanimous All-American, and the MVP in the Big 10. Legendary surely, but the legend doesn't stop with his playing days.

Harmon enlisted in the service during World War II. He flew numerous combat missions and twice survived plane crashes. One of those mishaps came in the Far East. He had to survive behind enemy lines on that occasion with the help of sympathetic resistance fighters. He was awarded both the Silver Star and a Purple Heart when he was discharged from the armed services.

Old Number 98, as he is sometimes known by historians of Michigan football, is without a doubt the epitome of what is considered a Michigan Man. His character and integrity as a person are truly his defining traits. As an athlete and player, his astonishing accomplishments will never be matched. But here's a little-known part of the Harmon story. According to Don Lund, the longtime Wolverine player, coach, and staffer, Harmon actually started his playing career in the wrong position.

Don Lund: *Oosterbaan was on the coaching staff, and he kept saying, "I think we ought to play Harmon at tailback." See, Harmon played about two or three games at wingback, which was the right halfback. And they kept debating, and debating, whether to make the move or not, and they kept asking, "Well, who will play right halfback if you move him?" Oosterbaan said, "Anybody." And he was right. You know, he was right about Harmon. I came up to see Harmon play when I was in high school, and he just did it all, let's face it! He caught the ball, he kicked the ball, he passed the ball, he ran the ball. He did it all, as well as anybody. He just was outstanding. It was all the under-pressure things too. You've seen all those stories, like when the drunk came out of the stands. You see, that was* *his birthday. That was the first team to fly, the Michigan team landed in Denver to refuel, and then on to the coast. They get in there, and here it is opening kickoff, and he takes the opening kickoff and runs for a touchdown. It's his birthday!*

If you needed any more evidence that Harmon was head and shoulders above everyone else, just read this from Forest Evashevski, who in his own right is a legend of epic proportion. Yet, Evy has Tom Harmon at the top of the mountain

Forest Evashevski: *The greatest thrill I had was starting as a sophomore and playing in front of Tom Harmon. Tom Harmon was the greatest football player that we had in the whole century because he ran, he passed, and he held the state record in the 100 in Indiana for 15 years. He was a good kicker. He place-kicked, he kicked off, and kicked our extra points. And not only that, but he was a great defensive back, and very few people know that he was injured—he was shot down in the war, and his legs were badly scarred so the doctors wouldn't let him play offense—but he played regular defense for the Los Angeles Rams. At Columbus in 1940, when Tom came off the field and we won 40 to nothing, Tom's jersey was torn all the way off and he had no sleeves on the jersey. That was the greatest thrill, because Tom, when he came off, well for all of us, we got a standing ovation from the Ohio State crowd. When you get that from them as a Michigan Man, well, you know...*

Harmon clearly dominated his era, even to the grudging respect of Ohio State fans. Less than 20 years later, another player came along in Maize and Blue, who was similarly dominant. While he didn't win the Heisman like Harmon, his number is one of only five to be retired from the Michigan Football program. His name was Ron Kramer, and he was number 87. He was a friend of mine. He was a legend. He was a unique, playful, rough-around-the-edges, outspoken and a completely lovable character. Nobody loved Michigan more than Ron Kramer; that's one of the reasons I loved him.

But more than that, he was maybe one of the best overall athletes ever in the 20th century. Ron won nine letters at Michigan—as many as were allowed at the time. He was an All-American in football. He was the team MVP and the captain in basketball, and its leading scorer. Ron was actually the Wolverines' career scoring leader in basketball when he graduated, and that record lasted for years. He was also a mainstay in the track team that won two Big-10 titles in his three years on the varsity. Legend has it that Kramer would finish his two- hour spring practice session with the football team, and then head over to Ferry Field, where he would change into a track uniform and win the high jump or the shotput, and help Michigan win the track meet.

All that being said, it was his football exploits that made Ron legendary. The incredible part of his story is that he came into Ann Arbor from his home in East Detroit as a marked man. His Herculean reputation as a giant talent preceded him. He lived with that reputation, and then amazingly surpassed it. One of his teammates as a freshman at Michigan was Terry Barr. Now, Barr was a pretty fair player in his own right, going on to an All-American college career and a noteworthy professional football life too. But when Barr got to Michigan, there was only one name on the team that the other guys knew about. And Terry told me the tale of how he got the great Ron Kramer mixed up with another freshman.

Terry Barr: *When I was going to Michigan with Ron and Tom Maentz, all the high school recruiting wasn't published all over, you know. I mean, so we had no idea who was going to be on our freshman team when we got down to Michigan. There might have been a little something in the paper, but I'd never read anything about it. I'd heard that we had this kid on our team that was an All- American high school player. And so, I go out to practice and there's this guy out there. He's leaping over buildings in a single bound, and you know, you stay out of his way. And he's mean, and he's all those things. So, I'm saying to myself, "This is the All-American, right here." I had never met him except I knew his name was Mike Higgins. So, I mean, if we had an All-American, that's the guy* *right there! I kept calling Ron, Mike. "Hey, Mike!" But he finally said, "Hey! I'm not Mike Higgins. My name is Ron Kramer. Quit calling me Mike." We had a bunch of guys on our team like you did, they were really good leaders, and that's what makes championship teams."*

Pretty soon though, nobody confused Kramer with anyone. He was so good. He stood head and shoulders above everyone else. Besides Barr, one of Ron's teammates was Dave Rentschler, who played two years with the great one, and watched up close and personal just how dominant Number 87 could be.

Dave Rentschler: *I'll tell you something, and I couldn't have more respect for anybody as a player and athlete as I did for Ron. And you talk about some people who are really gifted--I thought Jimmy Pace was almost as gifted, but not quite. Tom was a great player, Maentz was a great player, and so was Terry. But truly, Ron was gifted. He could do things that you just couldn't imagine for a man that size. He was one of the biggest players on the field. He could run with anybody. He had those incredible hands, and he was strong, and he knew what he was doing. One year against Michigan State, he kicked off, and got the tackle on the kickoff, and made two tackles--somebody else on the third down made a tackle. And then Michigan State went back to punt, and he went right over the top of Leroy Bolden, blocked the punt, and recovered it... Oh, absolutely, yeah! Nobody can exaggerate, really, I don't think, how good Ron was. Ron was really, Benny! Benny saw himself in Ron, and there was no question about that. That was Benny, back again, and Benny saw that. And you know what, Ron was such a good team guy--you'll never hear me say anything against Kramer, I'll tell you that.*

No question. Dave Rentschler was a Ron Kramer fan but you'll never meet, in this life or the next, a bigger Benny Oosterbaan fan than the great Ron Kramer. Benny was considered maybe the best athlete ever at Michigan until Ron came along.

Benny played in the mid 1920's at Michigan and he was so good during those years, he was named to the All-Time, All-American football team in 1974. But that only scratches the surface of Oosterbaan's impact in Ann Arbor. He was also a three-year letter-winner in basketball and led the Big-10 in scoring in1928. He lettered three years in baseball and led the league in hitting in1928. Benny was awarded the Big-10 medal after the 28th season, honoring the conferences' best in athletics and scholarship.

After he graduated, University of Michigan became his life. Benny was an assistant football coach for 20 years. He was the head football coach for 11 years and won a national title in 1948. He was also the head basketball coach for nine years. And if that wasn't enough, after his final year as the head football coach, Benny became the Director of Alumni Relations from 1959 to 1972.

No doubt, Benny belongs on the Mount Rushmore of Michigan Athletics, and he was Ron Kramer's coach when the legendary Kramer played for the Wolverines. As Rentschler said, Benny saw himself in Ron, and Kramer saw a special man in Benny. Before he died, Ron, who was a fabulous storyteller, told me about the head coach that he came to love and respect so much during his days as a player.

> **Ron Kramer:** *He was the most nostalgic and wonderful motivator as a speaker, a traditionalist. I mean, he was Michigan tradition. And I had such a great love for him and he never lost his cool. He'd never yell and scream at anybody--he had a couple of guys that he did every once in a while, you know, a couple of assistant coaches, but not very often. Benny was just a cool guy. In practice, most of the time you'd see him sitting over on the bench. He said, "I'm head coach, my assistant coaches can play and do things. I'm going to motivate, and I'm going to do these kinds of things." And he did have some good innovations off of the Wing T, and the Single Wing formation, you know, that's what we played when I was in school. We had to play offense and defense. Benny was always, Benny was always the kind of a guy that was very kind, very gentle, until the day he died.*

Benny, as Ron mentioned, was a gentle guy. He was not a fire and brimstone kind of coach--or player, for that matter. All he did was find a way to get the job done. On one occasion, he used his skill as a wordsmith to rally the troops in a pregame talk that Dave Rentschler never forgot.

> **Dave Rentschler***: In 1954 we lost to Indiana 13 to 7. They had a wonderful athlete named Milt Campbell. Now, Milt Campbell is best known because he won the gold medal in the Olympics for the decathlon; he was just a marvelous athlete. Well, late in the game, he caught a pass, and they scored a late touchdown and beat us. They just never should have. Well, the next year, we're over at the clubhouse and sleeping up over at the clubhouse. We come down in the morning and Benny was--they would feed us and then Benny would give us a talk—and the one talk that he gave us that I never, ever forgot, was he said to us. "Last year, we lost." (This is the Indiana game and '55.) "We lost to Indiana last year," and he said, "That should never happen." He said, "That's a heterogeneous bunch, playing for no common cause, and you guys are playing for Michigan. A heterogeneous bunch, playing for no common cause, and you guys are playing for Michigan. With the fact that you're playing for Michigan, Indiana should never beat you." Well, we had a great game that day. And I think we shut them out.*

Don't think for a minute that Benny didn't have a sense of humor either. Most coaches don't let their guard down too often in front of their players, but all of them do at some point or another. They're human, after all. Benny was no different. And Kramer recalls a story that speaks to the playfulness of the great Benny Oosterbaan when a couple of his players were, well, being playful themselves.

> **Ron Kramer:** *One fun time that I had at Michigan Stadium was when I was in school, they always left the gate open so that we could park with our girlfriends around the stadium. And at 10:30 we had to leave because all the girls had to be in anyway, and then they locked the gates. Well, my roommate, Charlie Brooks, one night--I would guess he*

was mushing in a little bit too much, you know--and he got caught in the stadium. And he had to climb over the top of the of barbed wire, go all the way over to State Street--South State Street--and wake up Bob Hurst and get him over to open up the gate. So, he opened up the gate, he drove his girl home, she couldn't go out for the weekends for a month. Four days later, Charlie gets this card; he's my roommate at the Sigma Kai House. So, he gets this card, and it's a picture of the University of Michigan Stadium. And you know, I'm a little nosy, so I turned it over and I read it. It says, "Dear Charlie, it's a wonderful place to play, isn't it? -Coach Benny Oosterbaan."

A wonderful place to play in many ways. Because Benny Oosterbaan never forgot the human side of it. All of the players I encountered who played for Benny, or knew him, spoke reverently about his kindness.

Dan Cline led the Michigan team in total offense his senior season of 1954. Despite that great year, Cline remembers that season vividly because of an interaction with Coach Oosterbaan, when Cline wasn't even in the game.

Dan Cline: *The one that I can think of was the last home game against Michigan State. I threw a pass to Baldacci that broke their back, he went 67 yards for a touchdown, and that kind of broke their back and then we went on to win 33 to 7. Then they pulled me out--Benny pulled me out with a couple minutes to go in the game. I was sitting on the sideline; the tears were running down my face. It was my last game, you know, for my career and stuff. And my roommate at the time was Jim Bowman, who was like a third string center, who went on to coach at the Air Force Academy. He hadn't ever gotten into a game, and I was sitting there crying. Benny came over to me and said, "What's the matter, Dan? What's the matter, Danny?" And I said, "Put Bowman in, would you?" So, he said, "Bowman, get out there!" and he put Bowman in the game, and that got him his letter and everything else. And he was so happy over that. But that's the kind of a guy that Benny was. I mean, he was a guy that you* *wanted to play for--not that he pushed you to play, and not that he was ever nasty to you or, you know--he was the kind of a coach that you would, you know, you'd want to break your tail for, not one that would break your tail if you--not like some other coaches have been, you know. He was just wonderful.*

Benny was, without a doubt, one of those special guys who understood a situation or a moment and acted on it. In most cases, it was to the benefit of one of his players or an assistant coach. Such was the case with a young Don Dufek, an eventual team MVP and All Big-100 selection. Dufek, who also fathered two All-American Wolverine football players, wasn't having an easy time of it in in Ann Arbor as a new underclassmen. As a matter of fact, as Don Dufek Sr. told me, he may have left Michigan had it not been for Coach Oosterbaan's benevolent intervention.

Don Dufek: *I was about to go home, without...back to Chicago because I wasn't eating on the training table or anything and my money was running out. And so, in the shower that afternoon, I just happened to be in a shower when Benny comes into the shower next to me, and he says to me, "Nice, going kid. You did a good job today, keep up the good work." And I said, "Oh, gee, thanks," I said, "but I can't stay more than another day, because I don't have any more money to stay and feed myself." And he says, "Oh, that's too bad," and walked out. And I thought—well, I didn't think any more about it. And then the next day, the next morning at morning practice, Don Robinson, who was one of the assistant coaches, comes up and he said, "Dufek, you start eating at the training table at noon today." Benny always had some good ideas for kids that had some talent in one thing or another. And he finally saw that day that if he gave me a little more leeway, if he gave me a little more chance to prove myself, that I could do something. So, it was kind of a slow start, but it turned out to be a good one."*

It was so very refreshing for me to hear stories about the human side of these great legends. With Ron Kramer, a legend himself, Dan Cline and Don Dufek speaking so glowingly about Oosterbaan, I got a sense that I was getting to know him a little bit. Near the end of his career at Michigan, I was lucky enough to meet Mr. Oosterbaan. When I was at Michigan in the early 70's, I had the honor to see him occasionally around the athletic building when I was there for my football responsibilities. But I don't think anyone knew him as well as the aforementioned Ron Kramer. After Benny had retired, Kramer visited him all the time before Benny passed away in 1990. And during my conversation with Ron, he related his poignant story to me about his relationship with Benny and his coaches' final days.

Ron Kramer: *Benny actually, not formally, but he adopted me as his son because I was similar to what he was at the University of Michigan. He was a three letter, three sport man--three letter man in football, basketball, and baseball, but I ran track. So, you know, he just sort of adopted Old Krames…*

Absolutely, there wasn't a day I didn't go to Ann Arbor, that I didn't stop by and see him. As matter of fact, I used to bring all my new girlfriends there. I'd bring my dogs there; he loved my dogs. And we'd go take a little walk, you know, because he had to get a little exercise. We'd take a little walk out in his backyard. He had a little pathway out there, and so we'd go take a little walk. I'd say, "Come on Benny, let's take a little walk." Then we'd sit there and watch a little television. He'd give me a few words of wisdom of how he thinks the coaches are doing and, and how wonderful the University of Michigan is, and how great it is to be part of the Michigan tradition and everything.

And then Benny got sick after his wife died, and they put them over in one of the homes and I used to go over there and visit him. One Wednesday I went over there, and he says, "Ron, I'm not going to make it. I'm not going make it." And I said "Benny, it'll be fine, everything will be fine." I left and went home, and I got a call the next morning that Benny had died in his sleep that night.

We had his funeral and we eulogized him--Bo Schembechler and I both eulogized him. Bo Schembechler thought a lot of him, too, because Bo used to sit and talk to him about tradition and everything.

And I was sitting home one day, about four days after Benny had passed. I get a call from the funeral parlor and he says, "Ron, I've got Benny's remains here. What do I do with them?" I said, "I don't know." He said, "Nobody has called me, nobody has taken charge. You got to do something with this." I said, "Okay, fine. I'll pick them up." And I went to pick them up. It was a box, about six inches high, four inches or five inches wide, and about 10 inches long, and it said on it, 'Remains of Benny Oosterbaan.' I said, "Well, Benny," and I looked at the box and I says, "I think I'm gonna take you out in the streets. You haven't been out for a long time." So, I used to go to bars and then put him on the bar... Oh, yeah! I'd have a drink, and I'd say, because he used to drink bourbon and water, so I'd say, "Can I get a bourbon for this guy?" and they'd say, "What guy?" and I'd say, "Oh, well that's Benny Oosterbaan. He ain't with us anymore." I'd be out in these local pubs and I know the guys, they would say, "You're a real nut." And I obviously am a nut.

I really didn't know what to do with Benny. So, I, quietly at the time, one day, I went over to his house and I said, "What am I going to do with Benny?" And I went over to visit his house and I sat and just pondered the relationship that I had with him, and the great love I had for him, and the love he had for me. And I took some of the remains with me and I walked through that little pathway that I told you about earlier, and I spread some of his remains there. And I said, "You know, I think I'll go over to Ferry Field." You know, they played at Ferry Field right next to the IM building before they played in the stadium. And I sort of went out there and I put some of his remains there. I went over to the baseball diamond and I walked around the bases, spreading a little bit here and there. And then I walked around Yost Fieldhouse and spread some there. Then they had the building, the Benny Oosterbaan building, and I went over there and put some over there.

When I was in school, we walked from the…from the golf course every Saturday morning over to the to the stadium, and down the tunnel and out on the field and then back up and go into the locker room to get ready to play the game. So, I took Benny from the golf course and walked all the way over to the to the tunnel, down the tunnel, around the field, then I walked up to the top of the tunnel with him, and then he was gone. To me, that's my great tribute to the man that I absolutely adored. He was wonderful, and he deserved to be everywhere that Benny is now."

PART TWO

PLAYS AND PLAYERS

Michigan Stadium does not provide the emotional connection to many of us without the players who we came to know as we watched them perform their magic every Saturday at the Big House. The question is, *how did they get there?* How did these young men become Michigan Men? As I spoke with many of them, the reasons were varied, but a consistent theme ran through almost every response. That theme was that Michigan was different than other schools. The opportunities at Michigan were perceived as unique, and the possibilities endless.

Curtis Greer came to Michigan from the Detroit Public School league's Cass Tech High School. He became an All American and first round draft pick after his career in the mid 1970's as a Wolverine. At the time, Bo Schembechler was making a great effort to recruit African American home-grown talent in Michigan. Greer and a group of young men in his recruiting class from Detroit started this wave coming to Ann Arbor. Greer remembers those young men in that recruiting class, and why Michigan stood apart.

> **Curtis Greer:** *When we came here as freshmen from the city of Detroit, from Cass Tech, there were six of us. Four of us came on scholarship-- Harlan Huckleby, Roosevelt Smith, Tom Seabron, and myself--and there were two other individuals, Tony Wolfert and Lawrence Crockett. Tony*

probably would have earned a scholarship but tore up his knee early on in his career. And to be able to play with individuals that you had great high school success with and then go on to represent Michigan in three consecutive Rose Bowls, and have a fabulous freshman class that we had with Gene Johnson and Ricky Leach. Those are probably the fondest memories that I have competing here in Ann Arbor.

There was a slew of talent that came out of Detroit during that time, many of them spent many years in the NFL. But it was really a tradition of keeping the kids at home and making a contribution to the university and, as you know, competing three consecutive years in the Rose Bowl. Being ranked amongst the top five teams in the country year after year and with that fabulous quarterback we had, Ricky Leach, it was exciting times and in Ann Arbor.

You know, it's not so much just from Detroit, but the kids from the state of Michigan. I remember coming on our recruiting trip, Ricky Leach and Gene Johnson was there during that weekend and all three of us kind of looked at each other and say, "Guys, we've got an opportunity to win here." Keep in mind, we had an outstanding high school coach. I can remember our senior year in high school, he kind of put us all in together. He says, "Guys, you can go anywhere in the country, UCLA, Tennessee, Ohio State, Florida. But I can assure you one thing; if you don't go together, you're not gonna win a damn thing. You will make All Big-10, you'll make All-Conference, and some of you might make All-American, but you'll never play for a National Championship unless you go together, because the concept of football is a team sport." It's something that we're very fortunate to have had that type of guidance.

And to know guys like Ricky Leach and Gene Johnson also went to the same high school was coming to Ann Arbor during the same time period. We could see very, very clearly that if we just continued to work hard, pay attention, and understand what Coach Schembechler wanted executed on the football field, great things can happen. And I think our record speaks for itself.

A member of that group that Curtis is talking about was Tom Seabron, another Detroit PSL product. Tom, who went on to a professional football career and later became a financial advisor at Morgan Stanley, told me about two meetings with Coach Schembechler that made the difference for him.

Tom Seabron: *Bo had all five of us in his office, and he closed the door and he said, "We're going to get one thing straight right now: I want a commitment from you five guys--you five guys are going to be the key to Michigan Football. You know, all of you are in-state, All-State players." So, he started with Rick Leach. "What school are you going to?" Rick said, "Michigan." Gene Johnson, "What school you go to? Gene said Michigan. Harlan Huckleby, "What school are you going to?" "Michigan." Curt Greer, what school are you going to? Curt said, "Michigan." Then when he came to me, I just said I don't know. Oh, and he went crazy. Probably the sign of the perfectionist in him, because he proceeded to yell, "How can you, right here in this moment with all of us committing, still tell me you don't know?" And I just said, "Well, I'm just not ready to make a decision yet. I'm not ready to commit."*

But probably the turning point where he and I had a one on one. We spent a Sunday at his home and at that time, my choice was I had signed a conference letter of intent. So, Harlan Huckleby and I had signed conference letters of intent to go to University of Tennessee with Bill Battle. And so, when Bo brought me to his home, he gave me a history lesson on colleges. He goes, "Well, why do you want to go to Tennessee?" I just said, "Well, I always thought I wanted to go away to school. And he gave me a history lesson about the black athlete. He proceeded to tell me how Michigan had recruited black athletes in the 20's, in the 30's, and 40's and 50's. So he gave me the whole history of Michigan football, took me through I think Julius Franks and some of these All-Americans that were All- Americans back in the 30s, and 40s, and 50s. And the Big-10 was the first conference to admit black athletes, and how can I be from Detroit and sit here, saying I wanted to go to Tennessee, in 1975, when they still hadn't had a real strong representation of African American athletes? So, it was from really that point that I learned a little bit about the South, because I didn't know anything. I think when I came back from that visit, you know, it kind of put Tennessee in perspective, you know, in terms of what was important.

Not that back then, race or culture was a big deal like it is sometime today. I joked with Bo you know, years later that he played the race card on Tennessee. And he laughed, he laughed. But yeah, he got me and I think he, you know, he understood recruiting more than anybody, even though he had the most phenomenal assistant coaches at the time. I think almost every assistant coach he had--if they didn't go, they could have gone--but most of them went on to be head coaches somewhere, and that just proved at that particular time just how great his staff was. But, you know, he had a way about him that truly made you begin to understand what he was building and what Michigan was representing.

It wasn't just Bo who understood the dynamics of recruiting, either. Bump Elliott, who preceded Bo, had his own methods on creating relationships with young men who were deciding on their choice of universities. Bump, who was one of Michigan's finest players ever--a member of a National Championship team and Rose Bowl Champion--was a gentleman's gentlemen. He was a class act from the get-go. I know because he recruited me, and I had the greatest respect for the man even though I never played a down of football for him when he was the head coach.

As a matter of fact, Bump was the coach who, in his last few recruiting classes, left Coach Schembechler a bevy of talent that Bo turned into two Big-Ten Champions and Rose Bowl teams. One of Bump's best players was George Hoey, a defensive back and punt return magician, who is still near the top of the record books at Michigan in the return game. Hoey tells the story of Bump Elliot's honesty making the difference for him.

George Hoey: *The thing that comes to mind for me is the fact that when I was recruited, I visited Michigan State, I had a call from Missouri,*

Ohio State, Purdue, and talking to Bump Elliot. And Bump said to me, "George, I just want to level with you. You know, we want you to come here, you're going to have a full scholarship. You're going to come here as a running back. But guess what? We have Jim Detwiler and Carl Ward in front of you. So, you're not going to play probably for two years, but we still want you to come here and you'll have a chance to get a great education. After that meeting, I committed. I cancelled my visits, and Dan Devine called me later and said, "You coming down to Missouri?" And I said, "No, I'm not coming, Dan. I already made up my mind. I'm going to Michigan." And he said "George, I can't fault that decision. But if ever you want to leave Michigan for whatever reason, you got a home down here, in Missouri." To me, for Bump making that kind of commitment, I mean, it's this pure honesty, legitimacy that I just bought into. And that to me is what represents Michigan. It always has and always will. Didn't blink. Didn't blink. And loved every moment of it.

How these players got to Michigan is one thing; what they did when they got there is another. One of the best ever in the modern era was Anthony Carter. AC was a smallish receiver from Riviera Beach, Florida who burst on the scene with a freshman year that left Michigan fans holding their breath. Of his seventeen receptions as a freshman, seven of them went for touchdowns. And Anthony returned a punt for a score in his first year and made one of the greatest plays in Michigan history, catching a pass with no time left and scoring from 45 yards out against Indiana that rescued a Michigan homecoming victory from a disappointing tie against the Hoosiers. We'll hear more about that play a little later, but in the meantime, we hear from Bob Thornbladh, who was Carter's position coach at Michigan. Bob, when he gets wound up, can get pretty animated and can cover a lot in a short amount of time. Anyway, Thornbladh is clearly one of Anthony Carter's biggest supporters.

Bob Thornbladh*: Anthony to me is…there's a handful of guys that are special. You know, I didn't see Kramer or Heston. I mean Kramer could dominate a game, and Anthony is right up there. We've had so many* *wonderful players at Michigan, but there--I think there's, you know, five or six and you can argue about them, that truly dominated the game. He dominated the game from his position because if they didn't devote two men to covering him, then we throw the ball to him. But if they did that, then we'd run off tackle and we had Muransky and Paris, and those guys. They couldn't stop us. And John Wangler, who'd hand it back to Butch Woolfolk.*

And that year, one thing I will say that I get mad about is they're always talking about, "Bo never won National Championships." Well, no one ever won National Championships, even recently with the BCS, you can argue that nobody--they play a game but no one wins, because, you know, we don't have a playoff system. And back when Bo coached, there was no playoff systems. So National Championships were not won on the field, National Championships were awarded. But with that team with Wangler and Mel Owens, and Muransky, and Paris, and Carter, and Woolfolk, we went out and beat Washington that year, and no one would have beat us. So, they always argue about who won the National Championship. That's like a sort of moot point because no one won on the field, it's awarded. Bo had several teams that certainly, if we had playoffs in those days, would have competed favorably, and I bet—I bet he'd have two or three in his pocket. As it is, he just goes down as the greatest guy and greatest coach that ever lived, anyway.

While Anthony was great from the start of his freshman year, it takes others some time. One of the greatest of all time was an unheralded quarterback out of northern California in the late 1990's. His name was Tom Brady. Now, if you remember, Tom Brady was riding the bench at Michigan until his junior year. We all know what he's done in the NFL. He is simply the greatest of all time, the GOAT, with more Super Bowl rings than anyone, and more records that will stand for many years to come. But as a Wolverine, Brady had some internal struggles that nearly derailed an historic career.

At one point, Tom even considered leaving Michigan. Fortunately for him, and Michigan, that didn't happen. One of the reasons it didn't happen was a guy by the name of Greg Harden.

Harden was hired by Bo Schembechler to be kind of a life coach for his football players. He became a guy who the players could talk to about playing time, and other things that assistant coaches, parents, girlfriends, and roommates couldn't really talk about. And Harden, in his own unique way, didn't pull any punches in his methods. Over the years, throughout the entire spectrum of college athletes, men and women, Harden has been a sounding board and solid advisor to some of the most famous names in Wolverine history. In Brady's case, Harden told me, it was a simple matter of convincing Brady that he was…well, he was Tom Brady.

Greg Harden: *The critical conversation is, "I don't care—" "Well, the new coach doesn't like me." "I don't care whether the new coach doesn't like you! I don't care what the coach thinks about you. All I care about is what you think about you, Tom." That's all that matters to me. I can't talk to you about passing the ball, I can't talk to you about reading defenses. All I can talk to you about is believing in yourself, win, lose or draw. And being prepared to understand that you, if you put football in the context of simply being what you do, and not who you are, we increase the chances that football will work. Because you're infinitely more than a football player in my opinion, in my experience.*

He had gotten the starting spot, and he was tentative and anxious. The good news, I mean, this guy was so coachable. Desmond Howard and Tom Brady, the most coachable kids I've ever met in my entire life. So, we're meeting like, practically every Friday before a game. And so, he's had a couple of games where he's starting, and the position is his. This is his junior year. But my job is to monitor, watch, and give feedback. I'm watching him, and he's so worried about everything. He's looking over to the sidelines, you can see that he's anxious and nervous. So, the breakthrough for me that I remember so clearly is we met, and I asked him if he was the starter at Michigan. He said, "Yeah, I'm the starter." I said, "Are you sure you're the starter?"

(Laughter)

"—'Cause you keep acting like, you know, you're worried about it. Son, you have earned this! It's yours! So, stop being tentative and worrying about what everybody thinks!"

Again, it goes back to, "What do you think?" These kids will follow you. And if you could have seen his face, you could see that his confidence was always growing. And at that point, it was clear, I say, "Bro, if you get taken out the game, you get taken out of the game. But you will certainly get taken out the game if you don't go in clear about your mission, and that you're in charge… That's all he needed! 'Cause he was ready. He was primed and ready to go, and he had trained and programmed himself to be the best. But as a real person…fear and self-doubt attack… Fear and self-doubt is the greatest enemy anyone will face in their lives.

So, how did it work out for Brady? I'd say it worked out pretty well. The result was fantastic but, more importantly, the transformation in Brady was amazing, even when it started to go against him. After his talk with Harden, Brady never wavered in his belief in himself or his abilities. His position coach, Scott Leoffler, remembers Brady's resolve in his last two years at Michigan.

Scott Leoffler*: During his fourth year, whenever he won the championship and came back for his fifth year, he was in a situation where he was fighting for his job from day one, that fifth year. You're talking about a guy that just won the Big-10 Championship, won ten games, and the first game of the year, he's fighting for his job. And I remember in the Notre Dame game at home, he started out the game real well—I'm not sure of his completion ratio, but I know that he was playing well—then Drew Henson was put into the game, and it was a standing ovation in Michigan Stadium. And whenever he was able to get back into the game,* *and led our team down to beat Notre Dame, you knew there was something special about that guy.*

You want to talk about mental toughness? A guy that just won the Big-10 Championship, and everyone wants Drew Henson to have his job. To go into that arena against Notre Dame, get taken out of the game, watch the reaction, win the Notre Dame game; I think that's a that's a credit to his mental toughness. His fourth year, whenever he went down to Columbus, Ohio—I actually mentioned this to someone not too long ago—the similarities between what happened to Tom Brady and what happened to Chad Henne down in Columbus, Ohio are very similar. And I think anytime that you go into Ohio State Stadium and get your brains knocked in for four quarters, I think that really, really says a lot about who you are, what you are, and what you believe in.

You can go back and look at what happened in—I believe is was the second week of the season with Syracuse. He gets pulled out of the first quarter, Drew goes in and does a great job and we win the game. This is a captain at Michigan that just got taken out of the quarterback position, and you would have never known that when he addressed the team at the end of the game. He's a team—team guy, and he's got "it" and it doesn't shock me one bit that he's winning all these Super Bowls.

From a player's perspective, there was no doubt in his teammates' minds that Brady was the real deal. Tai Streets played on the Wolverines National Champion team in 1997. Brady did not get the start that year; it was, instead, Brian Griese. But Streets told me he knew Brady, and his time was coming.

Tai Streets*: I knew right when he first walked in, when we first had them practices and three-a-days freshman year. Everybody was looking past him. Griese had a great year and Dreisbach had a great year. I mean, they were great, too, but you just knew. I mean, I just knew, personally, and always said Brady's gonna be great, great, great. You just give him the* *opportunity and you'll see what he can do. And he's still showing he's one of the best quarterbacks in NFL.*

Another quarterback who made history at Michigan was a young man from Ohio named Dennis Franklin. His historical significance is that he became Michigan's first African American starting quarterback as a sophomore in 1972. It sounds strange in the context of history, but at the time, it was a big deal. Coach Schembechler knew it would be a big deal, and he made sure Dennis would be prepared.

Dennis Franklin*: He pulled me aside after that spring game leading into the fall. And he told me, he says, "You know, you're gonna be my quarterback." And he says, "This is going to be—there's going to be a lot of publicity. It's unusual. It's different," you know, without saying that I was gonna be the first black quarterback. He just wanted me to handle myself like a gentleman, and don't get caught up in a riff-raff. And basically, that's—that was it.*

But the press itself, every time I did something that first year was, "Dennis Franklin, Michigan's First Black Quarterback." And that was one of the things that I wanted to work so hard to get rid of. I just wanted to be Michigan's quarterback. And eventually it just went away. He was very… protective is the right word, I think, particularly that first year. And then you know, by the time I was a senior, I guess being a cocky guy from Ohio. In fact, he was just telling someone—one of my friends—he's saying how cocky I was. But, you know, we all get over that stuff, right? I was just being me. I don't know! What can I do?

Players make history in a lot of different ways. Maybe no player made history in as many ways as Charles Woodson. He won the Heisman trophy in 1997 primarily as a defensive player at cornerback, but he returned kicks and played offense, which solidified his selection for the Heisman over Peyton Manning that year, who finished second. But beyond his incredible versatility, Charles Woodson was also a leader.

Legend has it that prior to the National Championship year of 1997, in a team meeting, Woodson was a key voice in that meeting that focused each and every one of his teammates on what they could accomplish that season. Team captain Jon Jansen was leading that meeting, and I asked him if the Woodson legend was true.

Jon Jansen*: The coaches leave the room; the captains go up to the front of the room. It was me and Eric Mayes—who hadn't hurt himself yet. But, and we're up there, we're going through our red-letter games, and how many first downs we want on offense and, you know, stuff that we had done with other guys for four years. The result was always an eight and four record, eight and four, eight and four, and it was, it was mediocre Michigan. So, we're sitting up there, and we're writing these things down. And they're like, goals are supposed to be…you're supposed to be able to measure them; you're supposed to be able to do all this. And Chris Floyd stood up and had something passionate to say about not winning championships. And then, Charles stood up and just said, "Hey, you know what? All we have to do is go out there and just win." And that's when Eric and I both looked at each other and were like, we started erasing the board and we put up, "Just Win." And I don't know…He just cut through the crap, yeah! It was the definition of insanity. We were going through the same process; we were going to get the same result until we did something different. And, you know, again, like I said, goals are supposed to be measurable; they're supposed to be attainable. You're supposed to be able to track your progress along the way. When you have a goal, one single goal that says, "Just Win," well, you know, we almost lost to Notre Dame. And what if we had? You can play the "what if" game the whole way down the line. And I preface that by saying, you know, when we went and told Coach Carr, Coach Carr didn't bat an eye. You know, and he was a guy that was very much into setting goals, and this is how you do things. He knew, I think, at that time that this team was going to be different, and there was something different about it. So, when we came with a goal that said, "Just Win," he's like, "Alright…Let's roll!"*

Woodson's moment in the team meeting was one of many he had as a Wolverine. You may have a memory of your favorite play from Woodson, but clearly one of his top-5 greatest plays was an interception he made against Michigan State at Spartan Stadium.

The MSU quarterback was seemingly throwing the ball away to avoid a sack. The pass was heading out of bounds down the sideline until Woodson came out of nowhere, jumped head and shoulders above everyone else, and somehow managed to keep his feet in bounds for the interception. As a broadcaster calling the game, I thought it was an impossible play. As a player on the field, defensive end James Hall was just as amazed.

> **James Hall***: I mean, we knew that since freshman year, that kid was good, man. But like you said, that interception against Michigan State…I was on the field. I didn't know what the hell he was doing when he jumped up, you know. I don't even know why he jumped, because the ball was going out of bounds. And I was like, "He's not about to do this." And he got up and he went up there and got that ball, man. I was like "Oh, dang," I was like, "He did that for show all the way." That guy made a lot of impressive plays his entire career and he took it to another level in '97.*

Since we're talking about spectacular plays, let's go back and revisit Anthony Carter and the game-winner against Indiana. Many of you may have heard Bob Ufer's call of that play; it's a classic! Bob nearly jumps out of the booth with excitement. But that play deserved that kind of call, and *nobody* could do it better than Ufer. The legend around that play was that Carter, as a freshman, ran into the huddle on that last-ditch snap and told quarterback John Wangler, "Throw the ball to me!" Now that seems pretty presumptuous of a freshman, but according to Wangler, that's exactly what happened.

> **John Wangler***: True story…he was leaving the huddle, he said, "Throw me the ball," and I said, "I'm going to." So, we broke the huddle, went to the line. And we had to…the irony—which I like to remind Bo on*

a regular basis, because of our sophisticated pass offense—we had to fake our off-tackle play to Butch Woolfolk. Indiana was in a prevent, and we were faking our off-tackle, you know, we wanted to hold the linebacker as we went through our 54 Pass post. They were at a prevent defense, which was fortunate, and he got behind the linebackers there and in front of the safeties, and that was really the open spot. We got the ball in the air and then Anthony did the rest. I was running down the field—actually to call timeout because I thought he was gonna get tackled and we were going to have to try and kick a field goal. So, I was right on the field to call timeout. Then when he got past the first guy, whoa, maybe he's got a chance. And then, then he got by the other two. And, well, I think it kind of took on a life of its own, because obviously we didn't hear the way Bob Ufer called it. I think that also really kind of immortalized it, you know, his great call of that play. And then I remember seeing on Michigan Replay the next day that they had like an insert of Bo and his reaction on the sidelines.

That was really one of the first times you saw that kind of emotion out of Bo, you know. It was pretty neat to see him react the way he did. I mean, you don't really think about, you know, the place in history or any of that stuff at the time. It was just a great finish to the game, and we were just happy to get the win and beat Indiana on Homecoming. I think, if I'm not mistaken, it was like the 100th year of football and a lot of people were back. And yeah, it would have been embarrassing to lose to Indiana for Homecoming, and for that kind of a game.

Now, if you need another source to confirm this legendary event, how about Bo Schembechler himself? Bo doesn't mince words and letting us know the story of the play is gospel truth.

Bo Schembechler: *Anthony told Wangler, "You throw the ball to me." And because what it was, was an in-route and see, by this time when you know you only have one play left. They're playing—they obviously played a cold zone defense and sat back there. The ball had to be completed underneath. Now if you're going to complete the ball underneath* *the three-deep coverage, who on your football team would you want to have the ball? Why, without question, Anthony Carter. And so, Wangler went back there, but in the huddle, I know for a fact that Carter told him, "Wangs, you throw the ball to me." And that's what Wangler did, and Carter did the rest.*

Another great walk-off finish at Michigan Stadium coming on a pass play happened in Lloyd Carr's first game as the head coach at Michigan. Actually, Lloyd was officially the interim coach at the time, and that first game wasn't going too well. Michigan was trailing Virginia 17-0 into the fourth quarter. It had not been a good day for the Wolverines. The offense had struggled mightily under first-time starter Scott Dreisbach. It was a blistering hot day, and the fans at Michigan Stadium had had enough of the heat and Dreisbach. As the game entered the fourth quarter, you could hear the boo's emanating from the seats.

You could argue that the displeasure of the faithful was directed equally at Dreisbach and Coach Carr. Many of the fans decided to get out of the heat and they left early, feeling it was a lost cause. Those who left missed one of the most amazing comebacks in Stadium history. Dreisbach engineered three drives in the last 12 minutes to stun Virginia 18-17. The final play was a walk-off TD pass to Mercury Hayes that Dreisbach will never forget.

Scott Dreisbach: *Every time I even think about it, right, and every time I watch it, it just gives—it gives me chills just to think about because I can remember it so vividly. It seemed like forever from when Mercury cut the ball at his feet in bounds, and then to his motion to come out of bounds—it seemed like forever for the referee to put up his arms for a touchdown. It was a great feeling for everybody that was still there; everybody still at the stadium just went crazy.*

It was a double shake on each side, you know, and I had Amani to my left and Mercury to my right The pre-snap read indicated Amani was the guy I was gonna go to and I dropped back, and they doubled Amani in my drop. I saw that they were going to him, so at the end of my drop, I was going to Mercury, and then I just—well I just put it out there and tried to keep it in bounds to let him make a play on it. But it was great! He ran a great route and kept his feet in bounds. And you know, it was very tight, but it was a great catch.

And then I remember after that, after they signaled the touchdown, I remember that our bench just cleared. And then the next thing, there was just a big pile—a big pile of players in the in the endzone. I just remember trying to stay away from because I didn't want to be crushed by anybody. Plus, it was so hot that day. And all of us—a lot of us had heat exhaustion and, you know, we're cramping up throughout the game because it was a very hot day on August 26th. I remember seeing the tape and, on the replay of it, I was just trying to stay away from the pile. I didn't want to get pulled into it."

One of the questions that came up for Coach Carr after the game was if he had ever thought of pulling Dreisbach earlier in the game. Lloyd told me he never considered it. Rather, he had a short conversation with Scott at halftime and he was good to go.

Lloyd Carr*: We were coming out of the dressing room and, you know, of course, we had really struggled. I mean, we hadn't gotten the first down. You know, I don't remember exactly what I said, but I did tell him, I said, "Hey, just find a way to win," and he did. Scott Dreisbach will always be a special guy in my heart because, you know, what he did in that last 12 minutes…I don't think anybody who follows Michigan Football will ever forget it, and I certainly won't. I mean, you're down seventeen to nothing. And I've talked to a lot of people that left the stadium. So, you know, he's a special guy in my heart.*

Quarterbacks and football coaches always seem to have a more intense relationship than other positions. There are a lot of reasons for it, but it's just the way it is, or the way the game has evolved.

Back in the mid 70's a relationship between a legendary coach and a young first year player, fresh out of high school, became a major story in the history of Wolverine football. The coach was Bo Schembechler, and the player was Rick Leach.

For many years, freshmen weren't allowed to play at the varsity level in college football because of NCAA regulations. But in the mid-to-late 1970's, that changed because of scholarship limitations and other factors. Coach Schembechler was well known for appreciating experience— heck, he wasn't really a big fan of playing *sophomores* much at the time.

For Bo to consider playing a freshman was big news, and for him to consider starting a season with a freshman quarterback moved the Richter scale on earth altering events. But Leach was a different talent, and Bo was a coach who believed in making decisions that were in the best interest of the team. Here's Bo on the choice to start Rick Leach, just four months after his high school senior prom, in Michigan's opener against Wisconsin in 1975.

> **Bo Schembechler***: The general consensus was to go with the veteran. However, I just, I felt that if it was that close that we had to argue over who the quarterback was, in the next four years this guy is gonna be something pretty decent, and we might as well get into it right now. We're playing at Wisconsin in the opener, and I took him around, walked around the track at the stadium the day before the game, on Friday, and told him that he was going to be the starting quarterback and that I didn't expect him to win the game himself. That he should take advantage of the talent that will be surrounding him and we'll do okay. In the opening game, he threw three interceptions.*

> *(Laughter)*

> *However, Gordy Bell, our great tailback, ran for 210 yards against Wisconsin, put on a fabulous show. We pulled the game out and won it, and the Leach era had begun.*

While Bo kind of downplayed the magnitude of his decision, Leach was well aware of the impact it would have on his life. Rick's version of his first start includes the ups and downs and swings of emotions for an 18-year-old under a massive microscope.

Rick Leach*: Bo never told me officially until we were in Madison, Wisconsin on Friday, mid-afternoon working out in their stadium. And I think a lot of that was, he had never told me officially, I don't think he wanted things to get more out of hand if they knew. I'm sure he knew how nervous I'd be looking at what was going to happen in the game, he probably didn't want to put more on my plate than he felt I could handle. The one thing I always remember when he says, "Look, you know other than me, here at Michigan, the quarterback is going to get more praise than he deserves when things are going well, and he's going to take more heat than he should when things don't go well. And I just want you to understand that." He said, "I'm telling you one thing now, and I want you to remember this: the only guy that you got to keep happy here is me. Then if things go south, I'll protect you and I'll do this and that." But he says, "You don't worry about what anybody says except me."*

As you know, my freshman year we won the first game, but then we had two ties back-to-back against Stanford and Baylor. And I'll never forget, I'm walking across campus, and at that time, Michigan had so much success that it was almost like a tie was getting beat. I remember walking across campus one time, and I know some people kind of point at me and laughing and giggling and I'm trying to think in my own mind, "What was going on?" Well, I picked up the Michigan Daily, or somebody put it in front of me, and it had a blind guy with a cane and glasses, and they were all already calling for my head and saying they could never win with me as a quarterback. You know, it was funny because you know now, I'm ticked off and frustrated, and I'm angry and thinking, "Man, I'm trying to do everything in my power and it's not like we got beat…although we didn't come out ahead."

I'll never forget walking into my quarterback meeting, Bo asked me, "How you're doing? You're doing alright?" And I said, "Well, there's a few things going on and I'm not too happy." He laid the article in front of me and said, "Is this what you're talking about?" He got a kick out of it so he started laughing. You know, after that, you know, everything stayed on track.

The one thing was, I can never thank the guys on the team enough how much I appreciated it, their positive reinforcement. Guys like Rob Lytle and Donny Dufek, kind of taking me under their wing and saying, "Hey, you know, you don't have to go out and win these games by yourself. You got great players around it. You just do what you do, and we'll take care of the rest." That's a good feeling.

History tells us that Bo handled the Leach era really well. His hard-bitten public exterior was revealed as a bit of a false front, according to his freshman quarterback. But the beauty of Schembechler, as I've always maintained, was his ability to assess people—to understand how to push the right buttons to get their best. Bo's relationship with Leach is a great example. After shepherding Rick through that traumatic and tumultuous first start, once the novelty had worn off, Leach told me it was back to the Bo he came to know and love.

Rick Leach*: I thought for the first year and a half on campus, my name was Dumbass. I said, every time I turned around when something would happen, Bo stayed after me. In fact, my freshman year when I—when I look back on it, in the practices and games, and sometimes I've had conversations with Bo, saying some of those things that we went through, is I look back on it now I said, "You know, I was competitive and played hard," but I said, "You've just stayed on me and on me." I said, "There was times I'd go up to the dorm so frustrated or upset that I was almost ready to cry." He told me—and I never looked at it then, and it, you know, just let me know what kind of guy he was because he said, "Rick, I know one thing. Number one, when you're the quarterback at Michigan, there's* *a tremendous amount of pressure in itself. Number two, you know, when you play in Michigan, there's gonna be ups and downs, and even when things are going well for us as a team and you individually, you got people nipping at you every day because they wanna—when you're the king of the hill, everybody shooting at you." And he said, "I always knew in my heart, if you could handle the stuff that I gave out to you, playing in front of 100,000 was not going to be a problem." If he could have told me that then, I would have been a little better prepared to handle it!*

One of the other factors that is part of making a great player is toughness. Rick Leach handled the mental toughness and physical toughness of his situation extremely well. And from a physical toughness standpoint, many players have proven their toughness by playing through pain and injury while still getting the job done. It's pretty much a given that you're never completely 100% healthy after a season starts. There are always nicks and bruises you suffer, but the prospect of not playing gives you recovery skills you never knew you had. Back in the day, injuries were attended to much differently than they are today. Listen to former defensive tackle Tom Goss, who also served as Michigan's athletic director in the late 90's, talk about his toughness experience in the mid-1960's when he was a player.

Tom Goss*: We went to Minnesota when I was a junior. I got double-teamed and I wore these arm pads on my forearm with my number, and as I got double-teamed, this offensive lineman pulled down on my arm, I pulled up, next thing you knew, Frank Nunley was knocked out, I was on my back, my elbow was laying off to the side, and all at once they came out and I said, "Where is my arm?" Couldn't find my arm! It was numb. And by the time I got up to my feet, my elbow was pulled out of the socket. That was the most painful experience in my life. I went to the sideline, and they put it back in and gave me two Darvon's. Now, that's when men were tough. Two weeks later, I started against Ohio State in Michigan Stadium, and Dave Foley had a field day on me with my arm taped to my body. So, you know, we did those kinds of things in those days.*

While Goss talks about "back then" being in the 60's, certain players are throwbacks to those days. One of the most amazing stories of toughness comes from a modern-day player named Steve Everitt. Steve played in the late 80's and early 1990's. And he was an all-American and first-round NFL draft pick, but at Michigan, he was the poster child for toughness, determination, grit—you name it! Everitt was not about to let anything stop him from playing center in the Michigan offensive line to a very high level…not even a broken jaw.

Steve Everitt: *The Notre Dame game, we're mauling them early on. We're playing Bryant Young; he was a nose guard. And I'm, like, killing them, my helmet's coming off, I'm, like, finishing blocks with no helmet on in front of the student section. Going crazy with no helmet, scoring touchdowns, running around and everything's going good. Then, a little short linebacker gets up under my face mask and shatters my jaw as Ricky Powers scores to end the first half.*

So, I ended up watching the Desmond catch—you know, THE catch. I saw that from the hospital with an IV. I rip the IV out of my arm as we score, like, cussing, cursing—like, happy cursing—but my mom's there, like, next to me. She rode in the ambulance there. They had to horse-collar my mom on the field, she was trying to run on the field when I was rolling around bloody. And she actually jumped in the ambulance on the way to the hospital and she was screaming at the chick trying to give me an IV to sedate me because I was going berserk. I guess I was trying to tell everyone I could go back and play, but I don't know how pretty that would have been. I mean, it was shattered. It was like a bag of marbles.

So, three plates and then actually a year later, in my senior year, I was out at Bennigan's with my parents and, like, start gushing blood and one of the screws had backed its way out through my mouth, but there was actually two screws holding the plate in there, and only one of them was found. So, who knows? Who knows where that other one is? It's still floating around somewhere in my lower colon or something.

We had a bye week, then I missed the Florida State game, and then played against Iowa the next week. So, it was like 20 days. I think that's where my—that's where toughness factor seemed to have peaked. I had a lot of injuries when I was here. I think I just had a chance to maybe prove how tough I was more than most people do. I mean, half of it's luck—just not having a guy fall on your ankle, like, two days before the Rose Bowl. That's what happened in my junior year. I missed three quarters of that game just because of a freak thing. So, I don't know that I was that much tougher than anyone else. I think I just might have had a chance to show it more than most guys.

Proving oneself in football can come in many different forms. For instance, two players in the late 1980's and early 90's had a unique ability as football players to leap very high. Vada Murray and Tripp Welbourne were their names, and the ability to jump in unison gave Michigan a huge advantage on special teams in blocking field goal and extra point kick attempts. There are pictures showing Tripp and Vada literally three or more feet above the players on the line of scrimmage with their hands outstretched even more, making it very tough on opposing kickers. According to Vada, the entire strategy was born from roommates challenging each other in their own back yard.

Vada Murray*: It gets to the point where Tripp and I kind of started to compete against one another as far as who could jump the highest. And Tripp always said that the photographers didn't get him at his highest point, you know, he had a second burst, and they didn't get that first. We lived together, so we go in the back, and we had a little basketball hoop and we'd settled it there. But it originated when Tripp and I went to Lloyd and said, "Hey, look, we—this is what we want to do." And Lloyd wasn't too sure about. So, Lloyd went to Mo about it. During practice, we'd try it and we'd try it, and finally they said, "We're gonna give it a shot." Then, you know, we started blocking kicks. I think the one team that really put a really good effort, as far as trying to stop us, was USC in the Rose Bowl. I think at the time, I don't know who the coach was, but he said they had* *players with broomsticks trying to block the kicks because they didn't have anybody who could jump as high as Tripp and I.*

Vada and Tripp made it tough on many kickers, but Michigan Stadium also saw opposing players make it tough on Michigan. One classic example of this was back in 1963 when the US Naval Academy came to Ann Arbor. The Midshipmen just happened to be led by a kid named Roger Staubach. Roger the Dodger, as he would be known, put on a display that few have equaled in Michigan Stadium. Staubach accounted for over 300 yards of offense and was instrumental in beating the Wolverines 26-13. He went on to win the Heisman trophy, and witnessing it all was Michigan lineman Jim Conley.

Jim Conley: *It was probably 75% of his highlight film for the Heisman trophy, and I can remember two plays. One, I had a beautiful back around and went in and I hit Roger Staubach and as he was going down, he flipped the pass off to a safety valve—I think the guy's name was Johnny Sai—and he ran for a touchdown. And then, another play—this is the one of most note—is the fact that I was playing left end, and our coach, Jocko Nelson, had come up with this sort of defense, and it was just, "Make sure that you trap Roger Staubach and don't let him scramble." So, he had the ends almost doing ballet, taking three slow steps and containing. Anyway, I took my three slow steps and all of a sudden had a shot at Roger, took the shot, and he went around me. I got off the ground and I went back at him, okay, and he cut back and I missed him again. And he went around the left end, and then I started to take a pursuit angle right in the middle of the field; I missed him again. So, I missed Roger Staubach three times on one play.*

Another play and player, that as Michigan fans we would just as soon forget, is Kordell Stewart of Colorado. If you are a Michigan football fan, you'll never forget the Hail Mary pass of over 60 yards as time ran out back in 1994, that defeated Michigan 27-26. Kordell Stewart to Michael Westbrook was a miracle at Michigan Stadium *for the other guys.* The Wolverines lost a 26-14 lead with under four minutes to play in that game. It was impossible, but it happened. And years after the event, Wolverine head coach Gary Moeller, in trying to analyze the play, you can tell he was still devastated.

Gary Moeller: *You know, to figure one of those plays out, you just have a hard time. Obviously, you can name a number of things—not enough pressure, the guy didn't go up to bat the ball down like they should—and the kids were waiting to celebrate. That's the hardest part about that game, the play. But, you know, it's the mindset that you've got to play every play to the end, and then, you know…it's not luck, but it is, to some degree. How involved is that? Because, you know, the number of times it happens…I mean, that's just a sick, sick day.*

Coach Moeller's view of the play was from 50 yards away on the sideline. For Michigan safety Chuck Winters, his view was up close and personal. He was on the field and in the middle of the scrum when Stewart's miracle pass popped in the air and landed in Westbrook's hands. Here's Winters' diagram of a play he'd like to forget.

Chuck Winters: *First I'd say in the first half, ran the same exact play and they tried and we intercepted—actually, I intercepted the ball the first half, going into halftime. So, we're thinking, "Okay, they come back this time, we knock everybody down." But now it was called a prevent defense. I was a swing safety. I was in the back, backing up, they run it down all underneath. So, we got Westbrook, Ray Carruth, and I'm not sure, it was one guy—Number Four—running down. And I see Number Four. He's the one, he's the closest guy to me. So, I'm backing up with him, I got him in my arms, basically holding him. Then, Ty Law is running with Westbrook, but he's kind of trailing him, he's underneath him. So, Ty comes in, the ball goes up, and we're both kind of backing up on our heels. We both go up, Ty tries to intercept the ball, and it bounced off his shoulder pad. And I'm, like, kind of right in the middle as we fall and it bounced in the air. I'm looking back, and I see Westbrook behind me catching the ball. That was the worst, worst feeling in the world, right there.*

I think it took me almost two weeks to actually get over that. Because it was just…seeing it on television every day. I mean, the coaches were talking to me about it, we have videotape of it. That was the worst, worst feeling in the world. So now, you know, I see it, and it's like, "Oh, I'm part of history." But you don't want to be a part of that history, though. Everybody was sick, and we just were sitting there in disarray, just kind of sitting around…Like it didn't happen! Like, we don't know what to say. But just kind of sitting there, looking around like, "Man, did this really just happen?" Because, you know, it's like, this ain't happen—this happens just once in a blue moon, and it happened to us. I'm like, man. You don't know how to take it right then. You don't know what to say, and everybody was like, "Man, it's my fault." And, you know, it was, kind of. You have to take responsibility on your own, but it happened. Now, when I look back and I see it, it still kind of hurts a little bit. But, you know, it's in the past, though, so.

While we are on the topic of heartbreakers, how about Michigan's Mike Lantry? Remember back in the early 70's when Mike was an All-American kicker for the Wolverines? I mean, Mike set records for Michigan, but he will always be remembered for the ones he missed. In both 1973 and '74, Lantry missed field goals that would have given Michigan the margin of victory over Ohio State. In the '74 game, he thought he'd won it, only to be denied by the officials in Columbus.

Mike Lantry: *We were 10 and 0, undefeated. Ohio State was 9 and 1. They couldn't get past our 25-yard line. Their kicker kicked 4 field goals, 12 to 10 with about 16 seconds remaining, and a 37-yard attempt. And I think it was good! Unfortunately, that's not what the ref saw, so. But that's circumstances. I mean, you know, we were playing for the Big-10 Championship outright, the birth of the Rose Bowl. And as you can remember, back in those days, if you didn't win the Big-10 Championship, you didn't go anywhere. So, all the marbles were all on the line all the time for us. Yeah, I mean, it was devastating. You know, to all the good things that we'd done, that year and then the previous year.*

From what my memory was, Tom Drake, my holder, we all kind of went up in a fashion like it was good, the ref—it was kind of a delayed call, because the guys came running out underneath the goalposts, you know, the referees. And it seemed like an eternity of delay, but they waved it off, right at the last second. I've never been bitter about the decision, but it was just, I mean it was heartbreaking for me, and for my teammates, because we were 10 and 1, ranked number five in the nation at the end in the polls and we were just sitting home, watching Ohio State go to the Rose Bowl, you know, so.

When I left in '74, I was third in all-time scoring. held virtually every field goal record that they had, still will always be in the record books for the first kicker to ever kick a 50-yard field goal. But aside from all that, you know, I was I was probably known because I was a Vietnam Veteran, and I, you know, a lot of people had compassion. It was just the era and time that we all grew up in coming to Michigan, just having a tremendous opportunity to do what I did, I was so grateful to be such a part of, you know, a team like the Michigan teams that you and I played on.

Yeah, I've made myself proud with the things I did. But, you know, unfortunately, I'm always remembered for those two kicks. That's my legacy. To be honest with you, I remember after the '74 game, there must have—the athletic department was getting kind of mad at me because they just kept getting tons of mail, you know, with all kinds of people that were just so sorrowful for me, and they just had to reach out and write letters and tell me how bad that they felt. You know, that built—built me back up and certainly, I was extremely disappointed in it. It hurt for a while. I guess it's in my nature. I got on with my life, you know, tried to draw some strength from it, I guess.

Happier times against Ohio State would follow, like in 1985 against the Buckeyes at Michigan Stadium. Jim Harbaugh was heading to an All-American career as quarterback for Michigan and as usual, the Big-10 title and Rose Bowl was on the line. But late in the game, it was a young, unknown freshman who stunned the Buckeyes and electrified the Big

House. As Jim Harbaugh stared down an unblocked safety blitz, John Kolesar was beating man-to-man coverage for a 77-yard touchdown bomb that Harbaugh never saw, because he was on his back. Kolesar, on the other hand, remembers the play with crystal clarity.

> **John Kolesar**: *Being a freshman and whatnot, you know, I didn't get the ball thrown a whole heck of a lot that year, anyway. My breakout game was a couple of weeks before in Michigan Stadium when Harbaugh finally found me. I had a couple of touchdowns and 150 yards receiving against Purdue. So, for him to recognize the one-on-one coverage, and have confidence in me now from the previous games to take it deep. He recognized that and threw it up and over. Ohio State had just scored on a fourth-down play, and a good 40-yard pass from Chris Carter that pulled them to within three points.*
>
> *So, it's about seven minutes left in the fourth quarter, and the momentum changed. Bo comes back first play from scrimmage; Gerald White goes up the middle for, you know, three yards. It's getting all tense, because we're getting conservative and we're running the ball. As a matter of fact, in the videotape, Musburger saying, "Let's get a little close up on the hitting that's going on," in prelude to the pass, because they thought that Michigan was just going to try to grind it out, get a six-minute drive. Obviously, they fooled everybody because Harbaugh drops back on a play action pass and took it deep. Fortunately, you know, Ohio State thought we were gonna run too, because they had, you know, everybody up close in the box. You know, they had man-to-man coverage on me and then Jokisch on the other side, nine guys in the box, and took on the safety blitz, and Harbaugh threw it up. You know, as far as I'm concerned, I think that was the loudest that stadium was that I remember in my career after I scored that pass.*
>
> *And in Michigan Stadium, you know, given its glory, and the size, you know, for some reason doesn't necessarily resonate with noise. I mean, there's some louder stadiums that carry less people, design of the stadium or whatnot. But that was the loudest that I heard the stadium when I was playing. Now, I've heard it louder since then, a couple of games, but that*

was certainly one of the loudest times. And Jokisch ends up tackling me in the endzone and said a bunch of words that I couldn't repeat, but he was happy...But of course, it was a big play.

We've been hearing about plays and players in this portion of the book, and while the reality is that players make the memories, don't ever forget that it is the efforts of *all* the players on a team that elevates it to another level.

Let's go back to the National Championship year of 1997. If you remember, that team wasn't a pre-season choice to be anywhere close to a national title contender. There wasn't even a clear-cut choice who would start at quarterback. As Jon Jansen, the captain of that '97 team, tells it, those issues weren't on the radar inside the locker-room.

Jon Jansen*: It didn't matter who the quarterback was going to be. And I don't think Coach Carr knew up until a week ahead of time who it was going to be, whether it was going to be, you know, Brian Griese, Scott Dreisbach, or Tom Brady. We had three great guys to pick from, and we went with the, you know, veteran, the guy who had the most years, not necessarily the most experience, and it proved to be a great pick for us.*

Brian was...and honestly—Brian had an issue up on campus a year or so ahead of time. Had he not had that issue, I really think that he may have been elected captain that year, which allowed me to be the captain and, you know, maybe I would have been the following year, I don't know. But, you know, he was a type of guy that had that that leadership quality, had made a mistake, came back, and earned his way back onto the team, earned his way back into what we felt was, was a guy that we would trust in any given moment, at any given time.

I'll just tell you one quick story. During that season, there were a lot of great stories, but the Iowa game—down 21 to 7 at halftime. Brian came in and, you know, we all knew that none of us had played a great half. And Brian came in and he said, "Guys, that was the worst half of football I've played maybe in my entire life, I'm not gonna let that happen in the second half." And we went out there, and everybody knows the story now. We ended up winning 27 to 24, and Brian had a great second half, hit Jerame Tumen for a touchdown, and the defense played great but, you know, that was the type of player that Brian was. That's why that team was so good, because we had guys step up at moments when we needed them the most.

PART THREE

MOMENTS

There have been so many memorable moments in Michigan Football, it would be impossible to even try and recap them all. Plus, everyone has their own moment that is unique to them. All fans and players have different moments that stand out. What follows are some moments that I gathered that stood out from the interviews with past Michigan greats.

Back in the late 60's, Michigan played at Illinois. It was another Big-10 game, but then again, it wasn't. You see, Bruce Elliot was playing for Michigan and his dad, Pete Elliot, a former Wolverine, had been fired as the Illini head coach the year before. As teammates, we all knew that the firing was not warranted, and we all wanted to win this game for Bruce—and for Pete, too. What happened in that game can only be considered karma.

Late in the contest, Bruce was playing cornerback as the Wolverines were protecting a decent lead...wouldn't you know, the Illini threw a pass his way, and Bruce picked it off and returned it for a TD. The saying goes, revenge is the sweetest when served cold, and this revenge for the Elliott family was sweet indeed...and as Bruce told me, he actually saw it coming.

Bruce Elliot: *"Actually, Jim, you may not believe this, but I did have—I did have a dream about it the night before. I'm serious! I had a dream that I was going to do something like that, that I was going to* *intercept the ball and run it back for a touchdown. It was pretty fast, although it seemed like a long time, because I was really tired. When I was done. I could see it. As soon as I intercepted the ball, I could kind of visualize that I might do something like that, I might bring it back for a touchdown. And it was really kind of exciting.*

I gotta give credit to one guy, Barry Pearson. He threw a block for me. I don't know if this ever shows up on the film or not, but he threw a block because I can hear him calling me, "Hey, Bruce!" And sure enough, I got behind him, and he throw block and I was able to finish the play. It was one of the great moments, certainly in my life. And I really appreciate all the support from the team.

What my dad also told me about the about the whole episode was that as soon as they intercepted the ball, the fans in the stands realized what was happening. All the Illinois fans were cheering...which is obviously a little unusual for the—for the circumstance, since I was a Michigan player. It was—it was really one of the great, great moments of my life. Well, I do remember a lot of people coming out there. As a matter of fact, it was so tumultuous that somebody was slapping me on the back and knocked my contact lens out. I kept thinking, "Oh, boy. I hope I have a spare," because I couldn't see much.

Other moments aren't as dramatic. As a matter of fact, some memorable events happen by accident...like this one as explained by former Wolverine captain Doug James.

Doug James*: My true freshman year, which was, you know, I was a five-year guy. We were playing Purdue and they had Mark Herrmann, and they were ranked, and they were coming in. That was the Rose Bowl season—Bo's first Rose Bowl Championship team. George Lilja was a starting center and was an All-American. We're playing Purdue, driving down field, and Lilja gets his jersey ripped off. I'm standing on the sidelines because I'm not getting in the game. And they're looking for Lilja's replacement jersey in the trunk, and they couldn't find it fast* *enough. Falk looks at me, and he rips my jersey off my shoulder pads, and he puts it on Lilja on the sidelines and Lilja goes back in and they go down and they score.*

I'm standing literally on the sidelines of Michigan Stadium in front of 105,000 people with no jersey on my shoulder pads. I had a buddy call me later, he goes, "I can't believe they put you in as center against Purdue in such a big game!" I said, "I couldn't believe it either, man, because I play defense." And he said, " Well, wasn't that you out there?" I said, "Well, it was my jersey out there and we pushed it in for a score."

As we embarked on this section, I quickly came to realize a lot of special moments happened during Ohio State games. Maybe that shouldn't be surprising, given the rivalry, but the Buckeye rivalry and its outcome can sure bring special moments back. Here is Mike Kenn, one of Michigan's all-time best offensive linemen, recalling a stunning moment in Columbus.

Mike Kenn*: They had a really good team that year, and we did also. It was probably to this day, out of all the games that I've ever played in, the hardest fought and the hardest hitting game I've ever played in, even in the NFL.*

It was 0-0 at halftime. We came out and I don't remember if they received the kickoff, or if we did, but if they did, we stopped them, and we got the ball around the 20 or 25-yard line. We took it, drove it down, and we scored. Kicked off to Ohio State. They moved the ball a little bit, punted back to us to like the 25 or 30-yard line, drove it down, and scored. Kicked back off to Ohio State. They weren't successful, had to punt back to us. Another 75-yard drive. Drove it down, scored. And Bo goes for two—he goes for two and we make it, it's 22 to nothing. We kick off back to Ohio State, they're unsuccessful again, they punt back to us, and we start to drive it. We crossed over the 50-yard line, and there's maybe four-and-a-half or six minutes left in the game, I can't remember.

But all of a sudden, we just crossed over the 50-yard line and Bo calls a timeout from the sidelines. I go, "What the hell is he doing, calling a damn timeout?" He says, "First offense, you're done for the day." Done for the day! So, I'm walking off the field, and finally I'm starting to take in the environment and the surroundings. So, I'm walking off the field and Buckeye Stadium—all of a sudden, I realized that it's dead, frickin' quiet. There's 87,000 fans in that stadium, and you can't hear a word. So, as I get to the sidelines, I turn around, and right at the 50-yard line I look across the field and there's Woody Hayes standing there with his arms crossed and that scowl on his face, and there ain't another player or coach anywhere near him, not even within 10 yards. I just said, "Holy shit." And we beat them 22 to nothing. The greatest game I ever played my life.

In 1997, after the Wolverines knocked off the Buckeyes in Ann Arbor to complete and unbeaten season and stay alive for a national title, Wolverine defensive end James Hall had one of those once-in-a-lifetime experiences during a rare curtain call.

James Hall: *"We went in the tunnel, went to locker room—saw those roses in the locker because, you know, that's all you hear about, is getting the roses once you go to Rose Bowl. Then we come back out into the stadium, the whole stadium was on the field, running around the field. We were just out there, with our peer students, fans, just celebrating and enjoying the moment. We had the Big-10 Championship trophy. We put Eric Mayes up on our shoulders and just carried him out. That was one of the best memories in the Big House for me."*

For safety Jeff Cohen, the win in 1980 in Columbus just can't be topped. It's a moment frozen in time for him.

Jeff Cohen: *We started out the season one and two, and everyone wrote us off. And we ended up coming back and winning the Big-10 Championship and winning the Rose Bowl—Bo's first Rose Bowl. I think the last like five or six games, I don't think our defense allowed a touchdown. The great memory that I have was going to Columbus for the Big-10 Championship,* *winning that game, and then in the locker room afterwards, I can still recall this visual that it must have been—but probably wasn't this long—but it seemed like for thirty minutes, not a single guy took off their equipment; maybe you just took off your shoulder pads and your helmet. For thirty minutes, it was just hugging, and screaming, and celebrating, guys getting emotional. That, to me, is probably the greatest moment that I recall, as far as in a locker room scene, was that. Roses were passed out to everybody, and you just didn't want to get undressed. You just savored that moment to the point where, when we got to the Rose Bowl, it almost felt anti climatic. It was great, but I didn't even feel the same feeling winning the Rose Bowl, than going down to Columbus.*

Because that season when we were one and two, and everyone wrote us off, Bo basically said, "You know what? We're going to shut off the outside world. We're not going to talk to the media. We don't care what people say. We're going to take the us-against-the-world mentality." We went down to Indiana—and I think they may have been undefeated in the conference—it was maybe the best team that they had had in a long time. Before the game, it was the first time I ever recall Bo gathered up the team, and taking the approach that, "Today, we're going out, we're taking over the stadium, and it's going to be our stadium. It's going to be Michigan Stadium. We're going to go out and we're going to take over the stadium." From that point on, the rest of that season, that was the mindset.

We're going on the road, we're taking over stadiums, and we're just dominating teams. And Bo kept reminding us, "You know, I told you guys after we were 1 and 2 that I still think that we're good enough to win the championship. Then if you just believe in the coaches, and you just work hard, and you keep doing what we talked about doing, it can happen." The thing that makes you really sick is we were five points from being undefeated and winning the National Championship that year. We're the best team in the country at the end of the year, but with those two early losses, we ended up fourth. That's my favorite season. I mean, it can't be better than that.

Clearly, the Ohio State game takes the emotions up a notch. And for former Wolverine linebacker Andy Cannavino, the emotions got the best of him. Andy related a story to me about Buckeye coach Earl Bruce meeting former Michigan linebacker Paul Girgash at a function after Bruce had retired. Girgash and Cannavino were teammates and remained close after their playing days, so Girgash called Cannavino one day with this story…I'll let Cannavino pick it up from there.

> **Andy Cannavino**: *My name comes up, and Earl goes, "Yeah, you know, Paul, I gotta tell you, that Cannavino was a hell of a player, but he's kind of wacky." Paul goes, "What do you mean?" "Well, he gave me the finger during the Ohio State when I was coaching." When we were playing Ohio State, you gotta understand, my dad went to Ohio State and played under Woody Hayes, and I only wanted to play for Woody Hayes and Ohio State, and they didn't recruit me or give me a scholarship—and of course Bo did, so I went to Michigan, and that's all I wanted to do, was beat Ohio State.*
>
> *So, we're playing my senior year at Columbus for the Rose Bowl Championship and all that. I am so emotional—I mean, I'm crying before, I'm so pumped up. It's unbelievable. I don't even know where I'm at half the time. I was just out of control. And there was a pass by the sidelines, and I dove, and I tipped the ball, and I rolled out of bounds by Earl Bruce's sideline. And as…when I got up, Earl Bruce was like five feet away—and I don't know what came over me, I swear to God, to this day—I got up and I just gave him the bird really quick and stared at him. And I swear, I'm not proud of it. I ran back to the huddle and I forgot all about it because I was out of my mind then. I don't even really remember. You know, I remember doing it , but you know, I forgot all about it until twenty years later, Paul brings it up and I guess Earl remembered.*

Apparently, the emotional stuff must come with the position. Ron Simpkins was one of Michigan's best ever linebackers. He just couldn't be blocked. To this day, he is still at the top of the Michigan all-time tackles list. Well, he, like Cannavino, let the emotions get the best of him before one of the biggest games of his life, early in his career.

Ron Simpkins: *We played Texas A&M. They had a great backfield, George Woodard, and Curtis Dickey quarterback. He was so fast, ran a 9.3 in the hundred and all that, you know.*

This was the first big game I've ever played in, and I guess I was just emotional. So, we're going on the field, and I just kind of lost it that game. I'm talking to them the whole game, telling them, "This is Michigan, you'll never beat Michigan here at home. This is our place." And you know, we're not supposed to talk.

We get back to practice on Monday, every coach, offense and defense, is asking, "Ron, were you talking on the football field?" You know, I recall saying a couple of things, but I don't think it was a lot. They were telling me, "You talked the whole game. Ron, we don't talk here at Michigan." I got lectured to by every coach, by everybody, about Michigan football, about what you do and what you don't do during the course of a game. I was just emotional, you know. They were threatening our territory.

In that same game as Ron Simpkins was letting his emotions get away from him, Ron's teammate, Curtis Greer, was having another moment. It was actually before the kick-off against Texas A&M in 1977 when Greer got the chills of competition that spurred him and his Wolverines to the 41-3 win. The catalyst for the pre-game emotion came from an unexpected source, according to Greer.

Curtis Greer: *It's right before we came off the field, running up the tunnel. Your thoughts are concentrating on the game plan, and when we walked into that Michigan locker room, it was just on fire. There was a level of electricity that I had never felt before. And it was really orchestrated by many of the walk-ons—the individuals who weren't really going to have the opportunity to play that day. They are certainly going to make their contribution to the Michigan tradition and the Michigan football program* *by supporting us. When you walked out on that field, you knew that you weren't just representing yourself, you weren't representing Michigan defense; you were representing tradition.*

While the walk-ons created a moment for Curt Greer, other moments were born from frustration or failure. On some occasions, coaches and players had real heart to heart conversations during games to iron out an issue or two. And these conversations worked both ways—players motivating coaches, and coaches motivating players to correct an issue.

Back in 1996, it was the players who rose up and took control against Ohio State. All-American center Rod Payne told me a story I had never heard about that game—and if you'll remember, it was the game when Tshimanga Biakabatuka destroyed the Buckeyes, rushing for more than 300 yards. The backstory on the moment that ignited that performance, as told by Payne, is quite a tale.

Rod Payne: *We love our quarterbacks; we really love our quarterbacks. But I think we I think we rely on them a little too much. My offensive line had Joe Marinaro at right guard, Riemersma was my tight end. According to Ohio State, they're ranked number two or three in the country. You know the offense line; our motto is, "Run the ball." Sometimes there's give and take from coaches to players. We went out, and had a nice little drive, and we were—we were working them, and we felt as an offensive line, these guys are ready to give it up. We knew we had a real big game on our hands.*

The coaches decide, in their infinite wisdom, to pass the ball. First time we pass it, it's an interception. We come off the field, mumblings and grumblings, "Come on coach, you know, we could—we could run the ball. Let's go." Coach says, "Okay, okay, we'll run the ball." We go back out the second series. I believe it was a couple of runs. Get a couple of first downs, call out a pass. Drop back...interception—second interception in the first half against Ohio State. Now we come off the field, a little more grumblings and rumblings, and say, "Hey, you know, you got the big guys now, and we're saying we could run the ball." Coaches say, "We're sorry.

You know, we're gonna run it, we're gonna stuff it down their throats, and we're gonna take control of the game." Okay, coaches, let's go.

We go back out there. First play of our third or fourth drive, we call a pass... interception. Three first-half interceptions against Ohio State. We come off the field and I'll just put it mildly to say that there was an attempted coup de grace. A mutiny from the offensive line to our offensive line coach, our coordinator and our head coach, and we refused to go back on the field if we throw another pass.

To make it long story short, the coaches, I think, got the message. We went back out and rushed for 400 yards against Ohio State. It was a day that Biakabatuka went 37 rushes for 313 yards, and our backup tailback Clarence Williams rushed eight or nine times for 85 yards. We beat the hell out of them! Let it be known that the smartest people on the football field—the true genius—offensive line, offensive line.

Running the ball is important at Michigan, clearly. The key to the rushing game, as you heard from Rod Payne, is the offensive line. In Michigan history, there have been countless All-American offensive lineman. One of the most spectacular—and pardon me if I'm biased because, this guy is a teammate and dear friend of mine—is Dan Dierdorf.

Just how good was Dan? Well, he was an All-American, went on to play for St. Louis in the NFL, was named to the NFL All Time Offensive Line in the decade of the 70's, and was enshrined in the NFL Hall of Fame in his hometown of Canton, Ohio. But it was a moment against Texas A&M in 1970 when Dan was a senior at Michigan that exhibited his greatness . The moment is remembered by long-time offensive line coach Jerry Hanlon like it was yesterday.

Jerry Hanlon: *They had just gotten wiped out down at Ohio State, something like that, the 55 to nothing. Then they stayed here in the Midwest and then came up and played us. And we kind of went on that field thinking this was going to be an easy game, and they had some good* *football players and kickers and they had a real strong team. They just got caught in a buzzsaw in an opening game. So, they came in here, and we just struggled and struggled and struggled.*

We were down, I think was 10 to 7 going into the fourth quarter. I remember—and I tell this story at motivational speeches every once in a while—Dierdorf came off to the sideline and he got on the phone. I was up at the press box. He says, "What's wrong, Coach? Why aren't we moving the ball? What's wrong?" And I said, "I'll tell you what's wrong! It's because we won't knock anybody off the line of scrimmage." Dierdorf looked up at me and he said, "Run the damn ball over me!" So, the next time we got the ball, we got it somewhere around our 20-yard line, we ran 26 and 27, which was an off-tackle play over our strong tackle. We'd go red 26 to the right, white 27 to the left, and we ran that ball behind Dierdorf every darn play, and we took it right straight down the field.

Don't give me—the other guys were blocking, too, but we put him at the point of attack. We ran it right down to about the two-yard line, and on the last play Schembechler called 28, which was the quarterback keep, and I darned near quit that job right then and there because I wanted to take it all the way into the endzone, run it and 26 and 27.

But as you know, by the time he faked it, Moorehead walked into the endzone when he kept it on the keeper. That was a defining moment when we were down and it looked like we were gonna lose the game, and somebody took it on their shoulders. A defining moment for him, and I think for the whole team because we then came back and had a great season.

Dierdorf was one of the best ever, and so was running back Jamie Morris. Jamie was an undersized back that his coach, Bo Schembechler, thought might make a good kick returner. Through hard work and an absolute unbreakable belief in himself, Jamie became the starting featured back for Schembechler and when he graduated, was Michigan's all-time leading rusher. Jamie's career is an amazing story, with some amazing performances on an almost weekly basis during his four years. But when I spoke with him about those great times as a Wolverine, he shocked me.

With all the records and accolades over his years, when I asked what was the moment he remembered most, he went back to his freshman year in a game against Michigan State and a moment I did not see coming.

> **Jamie Morris**: *I fumbled the ball. I mean, really, you're talking about a kid who came from—came from Massachusetts, who'd seen the Michigan versus Michigan State game from afar, and who really didn't understand the magnitude of it. I mean, yeah, Michigan-Ohio State is bigger, but Michigan and Michigan State, that's a state rivalry. That's brother against brother, all of that. I really didn't understand that until that game, until after I fumbled that ball. And, I don't want to say—I'm not putting the blame on me that we went six and six for the rest of that season—but think about it! We lost our starting quarterback and we really didn't have a backup, and that really just took that team in a spiral down.*

Not long after that interview, I talked to Jamie again and asked him, after reflection, if that moment still haunts him or if he's changed his answer.

> **Morris**: *We remember the losses. We remember all losses, no matter how small, how big, how big the game, with the magnitude of the game or anything. But the one game that I remember was against Michigan State my freshman year in the Big House, and the off tackle play that I ran. I got hit, the ball came loose, and Jim Harbaugh broke his arm. That was the change of our season, because we were pretty good. I think we were still a good team, but if we maintained Jim Harbaugh in that season, I think we would have been a better team. I think our record would have would have been better. I still look at that game and the things that could have happened, would have happened…different things like that.*
>
> *When you make mistakes, you learn from them, you let them go, and you move forward. When we come back and reflect, you remember it; it's always there, in the back of my mind, it was always there. But that helped me, that helped me understand that game, and what that game meant. Coach Schembechler would always say, "You have the honor to hold that*

football, we're giving you that honor, and once you put that ball on the ground, you lose the right of that honor." That was important. You don't want to be remembered as a fumbler; you don't want to be remembered as that's what happened. Being young, not understanding the game, you thought it was about you. It's really about that football.

Turning adversity into victory is the hallmark of champions and at Michigan, it has happened a lot for the football program. A moment like that happened back in 1981. Illinois was visiting Ann Arbor and the Illini were bringing in a very good team to face Schembechler and his Wolverines. This was a game that very nearly was disastrous for Michigan. Adversity turned into victory thanks to a couple of key moments. Long-time equipment manager Jon Falk was right there on the sideline and saw it all unfold.

Jon Falk*: Illinois went up on us 21 to 7. We had Steve Smith as quarterback, and I remember Gary Moeller had just come back from Illinois, so he was our offensive coordinator. They were getting ready to go up on us 28 to 7, when little Jerry Bergei, a defensive back, intercepted the ball right in the endzone and turn it around. Then the next thing you know, we marched back and scored to make it 21 to 14. Then we tied it 21 to 21. Then with, like, seconds left in the half, we were at about our 40-yard line and Steve Smith went back to pass, and I heard Gary Moeller scream from the sidelines. "It's an umbrella! Umbrella!" The defense, the backs, had kind of all gone to the left and right side. Smith ran 60-some yards up the middle for a touchdown.*

I'll never forget that, as long as I live. The feeling that they had in that locker room at the half and the way Gary Moeller had called that play, and in—screamed it out there for Smith to do that is just an unbelievable thing. We went on to beat them 70 to 21.

So many great moments like that come to mind for every Michigan fan who loves Michigan Football. To close this section, we go to a pair of very special moments.

The first was back in 1971. Michigan is trailing Ohio State in the final few minutes, 7-3. On the line is an unbeaten Michigan season, a shot at the national title, and an unbeaten Big Ten title. What happened in those final minutes is one of the most iconic moments in Michigan football.

Billy Taylor takes a pitch sweep and skirts around end for a score to ignite Michigan Stadium, and send announcer Bob Ufer into a frenzy, screaming, "Touchdown Billy Taylor!" over, and over, and over again. Taylor will never forget it.

Billy Taylor*: We had another play called and Bo changed it. It was a wide sweep, but it was just one of those surreal type situations where everything worked. I mean, the pitch was perfect from the I formation; Larry Cipa threw the first block in there. Bo rather threw a crack back block, and I remember following Fritz Seyferth around the corner.*

It was like, once again, my feet weren't even touching the ground. I was just running, running, running, and one last guy to beat. He dove at me and I leaped and stretched out and he didn't even touch me, and I knew I was going to score. And thank God the goal line wasn't any further away than what it was because I just, like, lost my breath.

When I crossed, all I could do was throw my hands up in the air and the stadium emptied. You know, that was our last shot at it. If we didn't do it then, we weren't going to get it done that day. I mean, I was almost suffocated by the crowd. I remember raising my hands to the sky saying, "Thank you, God," and the fans were coming over and they started piling all around me and everything—I couldn't even breathe.

I was fighting to get up from under there, but I never forget that moment. That was my last play in regular season offensively carrying the ball for Michigan. My senior year, it was the last game of the year, and it gave us an undefeated season. Who could ask for more than that?

In the same endzone where Billy scored his iconic touchdown, but 20 years later, another Ohio-native wearing the Maize and Blue stunned college football and the sell-out crowd at Michigan Stadium in a similar fashion. It was again against Ohio State, and the player was Heisman Trophy winner Desmond Howard.

Desmond was having an incredible year, and he was the odds-on favorite to win the Heisman prior to the Ohio State game—but you can never be sure. Well, Desmond left no doubt in the voters' minds following his performance against the Buckeyes in a 31-3 blowout Michigan victory. His 93-yard punt return for a score late in the game sealed the trophy, but it was his Heisman pose in the endzone that made headlines. And Desmond told me, the pose was not spur of the moment.

Desmond Howard: *Actually, it was brought to my attention earlier in the year. A teammate of mine wanted me to do something like that when we played up at Boston College and I scored four touchdowns. I wasn't going to do it then because it's kind of like counting your chickens before the eggs hatch. So, going into the Ohio State game, I said, "Look, I'm from Cleveland, this is the biggest rivalry in college football as far as any of us in the Midwest is concerned. If I get into the endzone today, I gotta do some special."*

It just came natural. As soon as I broke the punt return off for a touchdown, and once I got into the endzone, it just came to me to hit the pose. I don't even think Mo seen it when it first happened. He was just so happy that, you know, that I scored and everything. I don't think he really saw it. He probably didn't know what the afterwards that I did the pose.

PART FOUR

HAYES, UFER, AND THE BOSS

In all the years of Michigan football through the 1900's, there has never been an opponent of Michigan that generated as much conversation or consternation than Ohio State's Woody Hayes. For 28 years, from 1951 to 1978, Hayes built Ohio State into a football juggernaut. He was outspoken and opinionated. Woody is the guy who said, "Without winners, there wouldn't even be any civilization," and, "There's nothing that cleanses the soul like getting the hell kicked out of you."

He was a fierce competitor, coached aggressively, hated losing, and *hated* Michigan. Throughout the process of putting the books together, I found many voices telling me Woody Hayes stories. Some of it isn't pretty, but then again, we are talking about Woody Hayes.

One of his most outrageous outbursts came in 1971. Michigan had just taken a 10-7 lead over his Buckeyes late in the game. As Ohio State began driving for a tying field goal, the Buckeyes threw a pass intercepted by the Wolverines' Thom Darden. It basically ended the game...but Woody was incensed—he thought pass interference should have been called—he roared out on to the field in a rage. This whole episode is best explained by the referee for that game, Jerry Markbreit.

Jerry Markbreit: *I'm the referee, and I'm 40 or 50 yards away from the play. When the play is over, I look downfield and I see one of my deep officials, Lou Layman, signaling the ball going the other way. So, I know it's an interception. I come all the way downfield and I get over the ball and indicate that it's Michigan's ball, first down. I'm about to give the ready for play signal when I look over my shoulder and there, 40 yards out in the field on the far hashmark, is him—he's out there!*

I took one look at him and I reached in my pocket, pulled my flag out, and fired it up into the air, turned to the press box, and gave the unsportsmanlike conduct signal. His face was right on my shoulder. He followed me around for five minutes screaming and yelling everything you could imagine. Called me, "You little shit heel, you pipsqueak. You're going to change this call. You're the head of this crew, you're going to turn it around. That was interference and you know it!" Boy, he just stayed at it. For five minutes he followed me around out there.

Now, the security chief at Michigan—because it was a far hashmark and we were fairly close to Michigan—steps out onto the field. He says to me, "Jerry, do you need any help? Do you want me to help you get this guy off?" I said, "Just said leave it alone." Finally, his assistants came out on the field and dragged him off the field—literally dragged him off the field! When they got on the sideline, he starts to go crazy; he's yelling and screaming.

Then the first play from scrimmage, Randy Gradishar comes in and he hits the center with a forearm right in the face, right in front of me. Because I see the ball snapped, I see this shot and I flag it. And at the end of the play, that's an ejection in college ball. I ejected him from the game, and when I look to the sideline—because when you eject someone, you have to walk them to the sideline—I looked over and saw Hayes breaking the down markers, kicking the chain crew, and I said to Randy, "You're gonna have to take yourself to the sideline today. I'm not going over there. He'll probably kill me if I go over there."

That was the end of it. That game was not nationally televised because they had—I think they have a six and four year with that loss. But everybody

thought the game was on national television because that clip was on every
page and every television set from here to Timbuktu. He made me famous
that day."

Something like Woody's outburst had never been seen before and
hasn't been seen since. But on the other sideline, Michigan coach Bo
Schembechler, a former assistant to coach Hayes, was watching it all. Bo
knew exactly what the Woody was up to.

Bo Schembechler*: His glasses were steamed up, so I know he*
couldn't see. As I watched him out there, I said, "Woody, you know this
game is gone. It's in the loss column. But you're getting ready early for next
year." And that's exactly what he was doing.

Woody was, without question, one of the most complex personalities
that is so closely tied with the Michigan-Ohio State rivalry. His coaching
tree included many men who coached for him and then went on to
Michigan to enjoy great success and loved Coach Hayes. He could
be an irascible bully one day, and the next, he could be the gentle,
grandfatherly mentor type. Jack Harbaugh talks about how Coach
Hayes molded his career.

Jack Harbaugh*: To be a good coach, you have to be a good teacher.*
You have to be able to plan, you have to be able to explain yourself, you
have to have a passion and a love for it. Woody Hayes was one of my
heroes in Crestline, at the time. He said he could walk into any class at
Ohio State University and if you gave him two weeks, he could teach that
class as well, if not better, than any professor they had at the university
because he had that kind of a teaching quality."

And it wasn't just coaches who experienced the two sides of Woody
Hayes. One of Michigan's greatest players, Rob Lytle, told me a Woody
Hayes story that I could hardly believe, and in some ways, Rob found
hard to believe when it was all happening.

Rob Lytle*: When I got recruited, he called, because it was getting to that time and I had to make a decision. I had gone to Ohio State one week, I cancelled Notre Dame, and I had a trip to go to USC, and then I was going to Ohio State. He came up when I—when I decided. He came, drove to Fremont, met me at the high school before classes started, and made me look him in the face and tell him! He wanted one more shot at me. I had to sit there and tell him that I was going to Michigan. And he says, "I want to know why you're going to Michigan." I said, "I think that's a better fit." And I started on Bo Schembechler and he says, "Son of a bitch. You should know better. I can do more for you and he can ever do for you at Michigan!" And he said, "You'll regret it. You won't win against us." Then he turned around, wouldn't shake my hand, and said, "Good, we'll be alright without you."*

It was the damndest thing! Woody did a lot for me. He never talked to me. When I was out in Denver, Randy Gradishar used to always come up and say, "Here's a note from Woody." But he would never talk to me.

And the damnedest thing was going into my fifth year in the NFL—and I was done. By that time, I think I've had six surgeries. They sold the team, Dan Reeves gets hired, and I know he's going to clean house. I show up to minicamp and they'd traded for Tony Reed, who was out of Kansas City and had just come off an All-Pro season down there. I came into training camp pretty good shape and went through it. But I was pitted against all the new young guys, so I had to prove my speed and all this stuff, and I got through all that. So, I don't think I'm gonna make the team, but we're down to last cut. We're in our meeting before we go out for the afternoon practice to get ready for the first game of the season—we usually have a special teams meeting. Reeves is late. We're all waiting and waiting for about 20 minutes. Finally, the other coach comes in and runs the meeting and Reeves comes in just as we're about finishing up and calls my name. Of course, that means you've either been traded or they're releasing you because they picked up somebody else.

So, I come up there, hand in my playbook, and said, "I'm sure I've been released or traded or something." And he said, "Oh, hell no, you made the team, that's no problem. You made the team before the season even started." I said, "You could have saved me a lot of anguish!" then he said, "Didn't you play for Michigan?" And I said, "Yeah." He said, "The reason I'm late for this meeting is because Woody wouldn't let me off the phone." I said, "What?" He said, "Woody has been on my ass for forty minutes. I finally had to say to Woody, 'I got players waiting for me. I have a meeting.'" He said, "You've got one of the biggest fans a guy could ever ask for." And I said, "Well, what do you mean?" He said, "Woody called me to tell me that Rob Lytle is one of these guys that's got to be out on the field, playing and get knocked around." He said, "That guy who took on All-Pro Otis Armstrong and took on another guy that had the potential to be one and ruined their careers by running them in there for a play, taking them over there for a play, putting them on the bench for a play. These guys didn't know if they were coming or going. This guy can do this for you, he can do that for you." I mean, he just built me up to being the second coming of Christ! And he said, "If he doesn't start for you…" And Dan goes, "Woody, you got to understand, the kid is beat up. He's had four knee operations, two shoulder, he's been chewed up pretty good. We'll hopefully get some playing time from him. But I—I don't know if he can take the burden of being a featured back." He said, "Well, you're a nut if you don't." I said, "I don't know, Dan, that surprises the hell out of me." I always get stopped by Randy Gradishar, and he tells me that Woody says, "Hello." But I never realized that I made that kind of impression on him, but I do appreciate it.

Then I asked Reeves, "Did that help?" He said, "Nah, hell, you already made the team." Reeves said he had to tell Woody that I had made the team, and Hayes told Reeves, "Okay, fine, then you made the right decision." I thought the world of Woody. I really liked him.

Pretty amazing, but that was Woody. He was a complex individual whose public persona didn't always match up with his private life. His intensity and anger caught up with him in 1979 at the Gator Bowl, when he took a swing at an opponent player after a turnover. He couldn't survive the outrage on that one and was relieved of his coaching duties. But surprisingly, long-time Michigan assistant Jerry Hanlon told me a story I had never heard about the aftermath of Coach Hayes' departure in Columbus.

Jerry Hanlon: *When Woody got fired at Ohio State, do you know where he came for the first time after he left the campus? He came to Michigan. Bo called me and he said, "Don't go, don't have anything to do tonight. We got something we have to do." And I said, "Well, what do you mean?" He said, "We're taking Woody to dinner." Woody came and went to practice with us, walked around, and he talked to the team little bit, watched practice and so forth, and then he and I and Bo went to dinner.*

It was one of the most interesting conversations I think I've ever been in. First thing Bo says to him is, "Do you remember Jerry Hanlon?" "Remember him? Well, that little SOB? He's the only one that coaches like me on your staff! So, don't tell me I don't know who he is." And I wondered, "What the heck is this all about?" Because I'd never had any idea. I mean, we knew each other simply because I was a high school coach. And, of course, when we were in Miami, I would go up there for clinics and things. I'll tell you this, he was an honest, hard-working football coach. What else can you ask for? And he meant for his kids to be successful, too."

Coach Hayes was, without a doubt, the man Michigan fans loved to hate. He generated all kinds of emotions with the Michigan players. His demeanor on the sidelines seemed to dare players into actions they normally wouldn't take during a game, but couldn't resist against coach Hayes. Here's fullback Dave Fisher from the mid 60's on his encounter with the Ohio State legend.

Dave Fisher: *I got knocked out of bounds—this wasn't in our stadium; it was down in Columbus—I got knocked out of bounds in front of Woody. Being an Ohio kid, I wanted to beat him as bad as anything.*

So, we're going down the field, and I get knocked out of bounds in front of him, and I go, "Well, we got you, fat man." And I don't know why I said it. But that's what I said, and he spit at me.

(Laughter)

We couldn't believe it! We were chuckling about that forever."

Maybe no one on the Michigan side ever had as much interaction with Coach Hayes during the Ten-Year War, when Bo and Woody battled head-to-head, than Wolverine equipment manager Jon Falk. Jon always seemed to get in the middle of a controversy, or a logistical issue, with the Buckeyes' head coach. According to Falk, one year, it was about Michigan's shoes.

Jon Falk*: That was in 1977. We had that tartan field over there, and that was slick. When it rained, it was slick—just like playing ice. I remember Ara Parseghian called Bo about some football shoes that were made over in Canada that they used on the Canadian fields. Bo told me to get two to three pairs. So, I got them. And the last scrimmage before the season started, wouldn't you know, it rained! So, I put those three pairs on those guys, and those guys stood up and they were all telling me about how those shoes were better than the ones we were wearing. So, we ordered 150 pairs of those shoes. We flew them in from Canada and had them here. We only used them when it rained, 'cause they were way too grippy if it didn't rain.*

All season, I'll be darned if it didn't rain almost every home game. Teams were coming in, slipping all over the place. We were standing in there with our footing. And Minnesota, we beat them that year, I think, like, 45 to nothing or something, and they were just slipping and sliding all over the place. But before the game, I'd walk in the locker room, I'd say, "Hey boys, it's Tiger Paw Day, time to put those Tiger Paws on!"

Well, the week that we played Ohio State, Woody Hayes come out in an article in the Columbus Dispatch that said Michigan had secret shoes. He had been studying the films, he found out what the secret shoes were that Michigan had to play on these wet fields. And he went out and got them. So, Woody flew in 100 pairs of the secret shoes for our game with Ohio State. Same shoes! I mean, he studied it. He knew. He saw the films and he made some phone calls. I got the article in the paper that a guy sent me, and I'll be darned. When they came in to work out on Friday before the game and I'm walking up the tunnel, and I had the locker room door open, and there were some Ohio State players sneaking across the way looking at our shoes. And as they were coming back, everyone was saying, "Yeah, man, they are the same shoes. They're the same shoes." I had to laugh that Woody Hayes was that smart that he could figure out what was going on.

As you heard, Woody never liked giving the other guy an advantage. One season, Falk found out coach Hayes would not take "no" for an answer.

Jon Falk: *We had the field covered in 1977. And I remember, I had to be the one to tell Coach Hayes that the field was covered, and they couldn't practice on the field Friday. When he gets off the bus, I walked up to him and said, "Coach Hayes, just so you know, you are not going to be able to practice on the field. We're not practicing on the field either, because the field is covered with a tarp because of the threat of snow." He grabbed me and took his finger— his index finger—and jammed it into my chest and hit me about five or six times. And he says, "Every time I come to Michigan, all they want to do is screw me, screw me, screw me!" And I said, "Yes, sir, Coach Hayes, but I don't think you're still going be able to practice on the field." He went the locker room and I'll be darned if he didn't talk a doggone field guy—one of the guys who takes care of the field—into helping him pull the tarp halfway off that field, and by God if Coach Hayes didn't go ahead and practice on the field.*

So, I went back over and told Coach Schembechler. I said, "Bo, Woody came over to practice. I told him he couldn't, and he pulled the tarp and he practiced anyway." Bo just looked at me and laughed. He said, "He pulled the tarp and practiced anyway?" I said, "Yeah, he sure did." He said, "Boy, old Woody. He'll not miss a lick, will he?" I said, "He didn't miss one today because he practiced over there, and when we didn't." He said, "Well, that's okay."

Coach Hayes never missed much during his career, and when Coach Schembechler started at Michigan and became a threat to his Buckeyes, Woody was as vigilant as he could be to thwart any Michigan advance against his program. Even the recruiting trail was fair game to Hayes. Bo related this story about venturing into Ohio in search of high school talent.

> **Bo Schembechler***: You know, it was like this. I would be in a high school in the state of Ohio, and I'd be talking to a youngster for about an hour, and he's really leaning my way, ready to come to Michigan, and wants to talk to his parents. And I would say to him, "Now, son, I want you to remember one thing. Tomorrow morning, Coach Hayes will be in your school." And he says, "Oh, no, I haven't talked to Coach Hayes." And I said, "Coach Hayes will be here tomorrow morning." Sure enough, invariably the next morning, Coach Hayes was in that school, and it became a real personal battle."*

Despite the battle, in many cases, the guys who you battle with the hardest become the ones you respect the most. For Schembechler, that was exactly the case with his former boss.

> **Bo Schembechler***: I think that we both actually were kind of fond of each other, had respect for one another. We enjoyed the rivalry, and played up to the rivalry a little bit. Of all the eras of my career, the ten-year, Woody/Bo was the most satisfying.*

As much as Woody Hayes was the guy Michigan fans loved to hate the most, there was no question who Michigan fans loved the most. That honor would go to Bob Ufer. He was a student athlete at Michigan, and an exceptional one. In 1942, he set the world indoor track record in the

440-yard dash. He was a three-time Big Ten champion in the 440, and also played on the freshman football team in 1939.

But despite his heroics as an athlete, it is his broadcast career as the Michigan football play-by-play voice that elevated Ufer to legendary status. By trade, he was a wildly successful insurance salesman in Ann Arbor. But in 1945, he moonlighted as the "Voice of Michigan Football" for a small local station in Ann Arbor, WPAG. The rest, as they say, is history. His unabashed love of the university and his completely partisan, exuberant style on the football broadcasts endeared himself to every *"MEE-chigan"* fan who was lucky enough to hear the games.

In 1976, Ufer took his show from WPAG to the 50,000-watt giant, WJR Radio in Detroit, and his audience grew exponentially. For 36 years until his death in 1981, Ufer was, without question, the greatest fan—and most influential voice—Michigan Football has ever had.

All that being said, Bob's broadcast style and his impact at Michigan gave birth to many legendary tales. As a matter of fact, there may be as many "Ufer stories" as there are Schembechler, Crisler, or Oosterbaan stories. The *Voices of Michigan Stadium* would not be complete without a few Bob Ufer moments.

The truth be known, Bob really didn't need a color analyst on his broadcasts. The second voice in the booth just got in Bob's way. He was nonstop from the moment the ball was kicked off, to the final whistle. But there were men who had the job of being Bob's color man. Don Lund was one of them.

Don Lund: *I guess you'd say a color man—I think Bob Forman used to always say, "Lundo, you're the highest paid color man in history. You get a chance to say two words in the broadcast."*

(Laughter)

Ufer was very well prepared, but a character, as you know, and then his eyesight wasn't the greatest. Sometimes he would dream some things up, and Jack Lane, who was a statistician, and I would talk and say, "Do you think he's watching the same game we are?" But he really was Maize and Blue through and through.

I had one experience once. We're playing Wisconsin—the athletic director there, Pat Richter, ran a little down and out, and just as the kid is getting ready to catch the ball, a halfback came up and belted him. The flag goes up in the air and Ufer starts, "How can we win when the guys in the striped shirts are against us?" And he's going on and on and on, and he finally looked over and he said, "Sitting next to me is my spotter, or color, Don Lund, and does a lot of officiating. Lundo, tell him about that call." And I said, "Bob that was pass interference."

(Laughter)

You heard Lund refer to Jack Lane, who was Ufer's long-time stats man. Well, those two worked together for many of Bob's years in the booth, and Lane saw Ufer at his broadcast best. As a matter of fact, once, in Iowa City, Lane told me Ufer changed the press box completely to fit his needs.

Jack Lane*: Well, they did some revision in their press box at the University of Iowa. They fixed it so the windows were permanently closed in the booth. When we got there, we expected it to be just like it used to be; just request it and then they would take the window out for you. Well, they were really locked. So, I call this friend of mine and he agreed to help us—but he didn't want his name mentioned. He came down early on Saturday morning, and we went up there with a glass cutter, went around, and took out all the glass. Ufer says, "We got to get rid of it. Do I have to break the glass?" I said, "No, you don't want to break the glass." He couldn't broadcast the game without the crowd noise. That's why he had all the windows open. There were many times when it rained—it rained in on all of us. The papers that we had, all my statistics…they all got soaked!*

Anytime there was rain, the game was a mess. When we left Iowa, he told the guy to send him the bill, and Bob paid for a new window."

At the Rose Bowl on one occasion, the lighting wasn't just right for Bob, so Lane and Ufer improvised for the broadcast of the granddaddy of them all. Come gameday, the improvisation had unintended consequences.

Jack Lane*: You know, at the Rose Bowl, the game goes on late, 4:30 or 5:00 in the afternoon, and it starts to get dusk. And with Bob's eyes, which were not very good, late in the game he could hardly see. At that time, there was only one main press box, and it was up on the roof. For anybody else other than the official broadcast of the Rose Bowl, you were up on the roof.*

Anyway, we needed more light in our makeshift booth on the roof, so we went out and bought some lights. We went up there on the afternoon before the game, and found a connection on the wall to plug it in. So, we had lights. All we had to do was plug it in when it was needed at 4:30 or quarter to five, or something like that, late in the game. At that time, in the booth next to us were the Japanese guys broadcasting the game. We plugged in and our lights worked.

All of a sudden, we heard the Japanese engineer crash through our door, waving their arms. We tried to shut them up, but they finally got through to us what had happened. Well, we somehow had shorted them, and knocked them off the air. By plugging in our lights, we had—had ruined their electrical connection. So, during a timeout, we tried to tell them what had happened. Somehow, they got back on the air, eventually, but I don't know what they did or what we did. We didn't do anything! We didn't change anything, we just kept on going."

These Ufer stories tell you of a time when broadcasting was a bit different than it is today. Here's another one that came from a former player.

Tom Parkhill was a reserve and trying his best to find playing time any way he could. Well, for an Ohio State game one year, Parkie, as we call him, had one of the biggest moments of his playing career—but never actually dressed for the game.

Tom Parkhill: *The highlight for me, Jimmy, was making the travel squad to go there. You're looking at a guy that, for the Ohio State game, my role was not on the bench. You know, we only traveled 44 guys in those days. I was spotting for Bob Ufer in the press box when we beat Ohio State 10 to nothing down in Columbus. So, all the guys were freezing their butts off down there, and I was up in the press box. He was relying upon you to come up with a name of somebody that had made a play, and you had a pencil and you had to point to the person so that he could—he could get all the—all the information.*

That was my first opportunity even to be around an announcer like that. And, as you know, he wasn't too bad at what he did. I was just pointing out with a pencil—I think he recognized me as being up there once, but I said nothing. It was all very interesting. I did not make the travel squad, and somehow that's where I ended up. I can remember going down to the locker room afterwards with roses and all that kind of thing, and then Jocko Nelson, who was the wide receiver coach, said, "Parkie, you want to go the Rose Bowl?" And I said, "Sure." And he says, "Well, you're gonna be Oregon State's quarterback." I said, "I don't care, I'll be whatever you want me to be." And you know the rest of the story. We went out there and got the job done."

Ufer wasn't just the Voice of Michigan Football, though; he immersed himself in the program. Bob raised huge amounts of money to benefit student athletes' scholarship funds. To this day, an Ufer Spirit Award is still given to a member of the football team who exhibits great love for the Michigan program.

Whenever the coaches needed an emcee for a banquet, Ufer was there to add his unique brand of salesmanship to the proceedings. Jack Harbaugh remembers Bob's impact at these events.

Jack Harbaugh: *Bob used to speak to our team. During recruiting season, you'd have, like, six, seven recruiting weekends where—had a dinner and Bob would give the same talk six, seven times every year. For seven years, I heard this talk. And it had such a profound effect on me. When I tell the story, I tell it in memory of my dear, dear, friend Bob Ufer. There's a record that's a country-western song about a dad in the stands that tells this story, so it must have some roots to it. Bob Ufer would tell the story.*

There's a player in Michigan by the name of Billy. He's in his senior year and had never played a down in football, wasn't good enough to play on the team. They're playing for the State Championship on Friday night. He walked into the coach's office on Wednesday and tells him that he may not be at the game because his father had passed, and Coach says, "I understand, and condolences to your family and your mom," and Billy leaves. Friday night, about an hour and a half before the game, there was a knock on the coach's door. He opened the door and it's Billy. He said, "We've done everything we can do, and my mom and I think it's important that we be with our team for the State Championship." Coach tells Billy to go get dressed. "No, Coach, I need to ask a favor. I need to play in one play tonight. Give me one play." Coach says "Billy, you've been here since you were a freshman and you've never played a down. How fair would that be to your teammates playing for the State Championship?" Billy said, "Please, Coach, just one play." Coach said, "If we lose the toss and kickoff, I'll allow you to run down under the opening kickoff."

Well, as luck would have it, they lost the toss and they kick off. Billy's on the field and the ball's rolling down the field, and the opponent gets it on about the 5-yard line. Here he comes—15, 20, 22 yards. Boom! Explosion! Ball goes one way, helmet goes the other way, things were flying around. The coach says, "Who was that?" "Coach, that was Billy." So, Billy walked by the coach and says, "Thanks, Coach, thank you." Coach says, "No, Billy, you're in. You're going to be our middle linebacker tonight!" So, Billy plays, and they're ahead by about 3 points. End of the game, Billy had 23 unassisted tackles, 6 assists, had recovered a fumble, and caused one. But on the last play of the game, the opposing quarterback rolls out to the right, threw cross-country pass, and the tight end catches it—completely fools Billy's team, and down the sideline he goes, which would have been the winning touchdown. But again, on about the five-yard line, BANG! Billy knocks him out of bounds, the gun goes off, and Billy's team wins the State Championship.

They're in the locker room after the game. The players had all left—there is steam coming out of the locker room, tape on the floor, piles of pants and shirts on the floor, and all that. Billy is still in full uniform and helmet, sitting on a bench. The team had all left, and Coach sits down with him and says, "Billy, that's the greatest game I've ever seen any player ever play. Tell me, what did I miss for four years about the way you play?" Billy said, "Coach, you didn't miss anything." "What do you mean?" He said, "Well, you know my father died," "Yes, I do." "And you know and my father was blind." "Yes, he used to come out and sit in the stands when we were practicing." Billy asked, "Coach, don't you understand?" "No, you gotta explain it to me." Billy said, "Coach, tonight was the first night that my dad would ever see me play. And there was no way, no way, I was going to disappoint him, because he believed in me and I wanted him to see how I could play."

And what it tells us is that in our lives, all of us needs someone that believes in us. And we, as adults, and coaches, and parents, and teachers, need to take every opportunity we have to tell those around us how much we believe in them.

As Ufer entered his third decade as the Voice of Michigan Football, changes were coming at Michigan's Athletic Department that would shape the football program and the Michigan athletics into the next century. Fritz Crisler stepped down from the Athletic Director's job in 1967, and the surprise choice to succeed him was Michigan Track Coach, Don Canham.

Canham, an All-American in track as a student at Michigan, had just completed his 22nd year as the head track coach in Ann Arbor. He now had the job of leading this athletic department into a turbulent time and elevate it to its full potential. Canham knew that football was the key element in athletic resurgence.

In 1967, the Wolverines averaged just 67,000 fans per home game in a 100,000-seat stadium. Survival meant selling more tickets and marketing Michigan to the masses. Canham turned out to be the perfect choice. He was called a marketing genius and proved it year after year as Michigan's popularity grew. Canham's initiatives made Saturdays in Ann Arbor in the fall a destination and a must-see event. He hired a little-known coach named Bo Schembechler to lead the football program, and they were off to the races.

The Canham effect is still very evident today around Michigan Stadium. He is another one that is very worthy of being on the Mount Rushmore of Michigan Athletics. As he grew into the job and made it his own, Canham became known simply as "The Boss."

But it wasn't always easy—there were struggles in the early going. Before he died, Don told me of the problems he had to deal with because of the political climate in the country in those early years as Athletic Director.

Don Canham*: The terrorism thing reminded me so much of the Vietnam War situation. Every day, we get—I mean, every day, during the week—we'd get a phone call from some nut saying, "We're going to put a bomb in the stadium." So, Don Lund had a crew, and on Thursday, we'd start to sweep the stadium. We'd check the restrooms, concession stands, and we did it all the way up to game time. So, we knew that there were no bombs in the place. And so, we'd go to the stadium, and we'd get a phone call in the press box, and the FBI would tell me that we've got a threat, and they'd get all excited. They didn't know what the hell we were doing. But they'd say, "This looks like a serious threat." I said, "What do you think we should do?" Then they'd say, "Oh, we don't make that decision. That's up to you." Here I am in the press box with my family and the FBI telling me we have a serious threat. And some stadiums, at that time, actually cleared the stadium, and a lot of baseball parks did, too. But we swept it, so we knew it was clean. I never really had that much worry.*

Canham was the picture of cool during his tenure at Michigan. He appeared unflappable and handled any issue so smoothly, you'd thought he had a playbook in his head on how to handle anything. But what you may not know was that he was a nervous wreck during football games. So nervous, as a matter of fact, he wouldn't even stay for the entire game.

Don Canham: *All the time! And Elroy Hirsch, the Wisconsin Athletic Director—every time Wisconsin was here, Elroy would say, "Canham, what time are we leaving?" And we'd go drive out to my factory and watch the game on television. I was so nervous. And during the first quarter, I had to leave the game because I knew all the injuries, and I knew how important one game was because we were fighting, in those days, for our financial lives. If we made a bowl game, boy, that was gravy! And we could only make one bowl game at that time. Yeah, there were times when I didn't see much of the season.*

Don had a reputation of being a bit of a miser, also—well, let's call it like it was, many thought he was cheap. I prefer to call him fiscally responsible. But one thing that is very clear about the Boss; he made sure his teams had what it took to compete. Listen to this story from football equipment man, Jon Falk.

Jon Falk: *It's 1976. We hadn't beaten Ohio State in Columbus since Bo had been here. But I'm a son of a gun, if he doesn't call me in August. He says, "Falk, they have a kicker down there at Ohio State by name of Tom Skladany. He punts the ball to the moon. How are we going to return those punts, because they're so arching high? We don't have anybody who can kick like that. How are we going to return those punts?" I say, "Bo, I have a kicking machine called a Jugs Machine. I'll order that." And I did. And every 15 minutes, every day, we pushed that ball through that machine. We practiced the Michigan return team against the Ohio State punt team every day. Return that punt, return that punt. Jimmy Smith was back there every day, bringing it back 10, 15, 20 yards.*

And one day I got a phone call from the athletic director's office, Don Canham. The secretary said. "Jon, you better come down and see Mr. Canham because he's pretty upset." I say, "What's he upset about?" She says, "I don't know, but he's really mad." So, I walked into his office and I said, "What's up, Mr. Canham?" He answers, "What is a Jugs Machine and who told you to spend $10,000 to get that machine?" I said, "Mr. Canham, they have a kicker down at Ohio State by the name of Tom Skladany. He punts the ball to the moon, and we got to learn to bring it back. Now Mr. Canham, if somebody walked into your office and said, 'Hey, if you could buy the moon to beat Ohio State,' what would you do?" Canham looked at me and said, "Pay the bill!"

So, we got down there and true to form, he was punting that ball out of the sky, and true to form, Jimmy Smith bringing it back every day. We ended up beating those guys that day, 22 to nothing. It was just a great win, and I'll never forget—right at end of the first half—we intercepted a pass in the endzone in a tie game, nothing to nothing. We ran into that locker room, and I was going around telling them, "Men, this is it. This is our chance to go to the Rose Bowl! This is it." Just then, Bo walked in. And he says, "Men, that game out there, it's over today. It's going to be Michigan today, men! It's going to be Michigan. We just made Woody Hayes pass the football."

That investment in the kicking machine turned out to be a bargain for Canham and the football program thanks to the win over Ohio State. But maybe the biggest bargain in Canham's career came in 1969. He hired the unknown Schembechler to lead the football program in a clandestine and old-school, bargain-basement adventure that Bo remembers fondly.

Bo Schembechler*: I accepted the job. I came up here, and as you know, he put me in a motel under an assumed name. And while we were riding in from the airport, I asked him, "What are you going to pay for this job? He said, "Oh, well, $21,000." Well, at that time, I was making $19,000 with $1,000 raise coming in the next year, so I'd have made $20,000. So, I came here, really, for $1,000 raise. And I said, "Well,* *how long? What kind of contract do I have here?" He said, "You've got five years. Do you want something written?" I said, "No, just tell me what the deal is." He said, "You got five years" And I said, "By that time, you'll know whether I can coach or not." And that's the way I came to Michigan.*

Like any boss, he had to be tough at times—even on a poor stadium public address announcer. Howard King was that PA announcer on a snowy Saturday in Ann Arbor, when the Boss came to visit.

Howard King: *I'm in my chair, and I'm right in the middle of calling a play—or the play was over. I'm calling the runner, the tackle, and so on, when I hear this voice right over my head, right behind, me say, "Tell them not to throw the snowballs." So, I finished up what I was saying, and I was annoyed by this. I had no idea who it was. This is early on, so I didn't know everybody's voice yet. I turned around and here's Canham with his nose right up to mine. "Tell them not to throw the goddamn snowballs." And I said something like, "Well, Don, if we do that, it's going to make it worse, not better." And he glared at me, and said, "Tell them to stop throwing the damn snowballs!" So, I cobbled up a quick ad lib that was very soft and gentle, kind of new-age, something like, "Please, in consideration of others and your grandmother," a "someone-might-be-injured" announcement, and Canham stomped out. He didn't think that was tough enough, but he left me alone.*

Back in the winter of 1969, it wasn't snowballs Canham was concerned with, though. It was his newly hired football coaching staff. According to Dick Hunter, one of the assistant coaches Bo brought with him from Miami of Ohio, Canham had an interesting session with the coaching staff at a bowling alley bar called Colonial Lanes, near the athletic offices. According to Hunter, it was a no-holds-barred Canham that day.

Dick Hunter: *When Canham hired Schembechler, Bo demanded that six of us assistants come in with him. I guess Canham just raise all* *kinds of hell and said, "No, you gotta hire some Michigan guys." And I remember Bo came back and talked to all of us. And he says, "Well, I'm not going if I can't bring all six of you guys with me." So, he gave Canham the ultimatum, so Canham gave in. Well, we got up there—I think January 2nd or 3rd—and then about the end of January, Canham said to all six of us assistant coaches, "Let's go down to Colonial Lanes, I want to talk to you guys."*

So, we went down in Colonial Lanes, and Canham says, "You know, I didn't want to hire you guys, and Bo forced me to hire you. But let me tell you one thing; I've received so many calls, nasty calls, that I didn't hire any Michigan guys. And you know what? If you guys don't win. I'm gonna have to fire your ass right away." We're all sitting there, then Canham had a beer with us, and he chatted and chatted. And he says, "Now, just remember what I told you guys." When he leaves, I'm like, "Holy crap!" Then we have a great game against Ohio State, and everything turned out well, and Canham said that it was the greatest thing that ever happened to him, was when he hired Bo Schembechler and bringing all six of us guys too.

He was unique, tough, kind, extremely talented, loved as an executive, and one of Michigan athletics' all-time greatest personalities. Don Canham pretty much did it all during his time at Michigan. But there was one occasion when even the Boss couldn't account for the Cub Scouts.

Don Canham: *We had a guy named Vern Rose, who was active in Cub Scouts. He printed all of our football tickets at that time. We told him that Northwestern was going to be the homecoming game, so you can bring the Cub Scouts. He printed them for the Purdue game, and Purdue had a hot team. We had a sellout situation and 9000 Boy Scouts came in. So, I got a hold of Bob Flora and I said, "Flora, we've got some kind of mess here." Flora tells me, "I didn't t know that the Cub Scouts were coming in." I said, "Okay, get some people and spread the Cub Scouts out all over the stadium. Let them sit in the aisles." And he did. People put them on their laps and such. We set an attendance record of 109,000, but we couldn't claim it.*

PART FIVE

GAMES AND THE '69 UPSET

We all have memories from Michigan Stadium of our favorite games, or games that, for a number of reasons, you just can't ever forget. When I go through my memory bank, I give those games a name. For instance, in 2004, Braylon Edwards almost singlehandedly beat Michigan State in a comeback win for the ages. I call it "the Braylon Game." Trailing 27-10 with just 8:43 to play, Michigan roared back against the Spartans for 17 points to tie it, and then won it in triple overtime, 45-37. Edwards accounted for 18 of Michigan's final 32 points. He caught 11 passes for 189 yards, and three touchdowns from Chad Henne. For Braylon Edwards, that game reverted back to playground football in the final furious minutes.

> **Braylon Edwards**: *It was definitely, like, you draw something in dirt and you say, "You do this, you do this, and Braylon, you just go deep, and we're going to throw it to you," and that's exactly what happened. They threw the ball up and I scored a touchdown. "Right strong, Braylon, go deep." It felt great to be a part of it. You know, I felt that I had a helping hand in that. To be a part of the win like that in Michigan Stadium...I don't think the fans, or the players will ever forget that.*

Another player who imprinted his name on a number of games was Desmond Howard. 13 years prior to Braylon's game against MSU,

Howard had one against Notre Dame—I call it "the Notre Dame Game Catch." It was fourth down, Michigan is hanging on to a precarious lead. Gary Moeller is rolling the dice on this 4th down from the Irish 25-yard line. Get the first down, go for the field goal, or what? Quarterback Elvis Grbac and Desmond were the key players, and what happened next became historic—and it didn't go according to the script, according to Moeller.

Gary Moeller: *He's gonna run off tackle, okay. Or we're going to throw a hitch. Desmond's going down, 5 yards, and turn around because they got off coverage. So, if he's got single coverage, and he's out there by himself. So, if it's off coverage, just have Desmond go down, hitch, turn around, throw him the ball, and get first down.*

So, Elvis is into this thing, and the next thing you know, they aren't in that coverage—camouflaged it just a little bit. I think he should have detected it. While he checks to the pass, the corner rolls up. When you got a hitch route on and he rolls up, Desmond runs a fade. As he rolls up late, Elvis went back with the idea that he was going to throw him the hitch, and he saw Desmond take off. You know, the one thing they could do, is they could connect on that, and just a beautiful throw—and what a wonderful catch. I mean, you're talking about a guy that just laid out. That was one great play, in a great game against a great team.

As for Desmond, he confirmed the Moeller story with the attitude that, "Hey, all's well that ends well."

Desmond Howard: *We weren't sure if we were gonna stick with it, because they rolled the cover to a coverage two. And I came off the ball, and I kind of came off hard, and I looked and saw Elvis was cocking to throw, and I said, "Okay, he's gonna stick with the play." And I just, you know, ran as hard as I could, as fast as I could, and looked up, and the ball was still overthrown. So, I just stretched out, as best as I could, and was blessed with a heck of a diving catch. Everyone was so happy and so* *excited because, you know, that was the first time we've beaten them in a long time, and it was such an exciting win! You know, no one really placed a lot of emphasis on the play call. It was a little bit of confusion, but it ended up well.*

Another game I will never forget was the Sugar Bowl game against Auburn. It was 1984, and Auburn had their sights on the national title. They also had Bo Jackson. In addition, they had running backs Tommy Agee and Lionel James in the same wishbone backfield. *Unstoppable* was the adjective used to describe that offensive attack with three future-NFL running backs in the same backfield at the same time.

And yet, Michigan's defense held Auburn out of the endzone that game. They could only dent the Wolverine defense for 3 field goals, but it was enough to win it 9-7. The Tigers would win the National Title with the victory. But, for my money, it was one of the most amazing defensive performances I have ever witnessed. While it came in a loss, it was no less impressive.

One of the guys who spent all night chasing and hammering Bo Jackson was Wolverine linebacker Tom Hassell. It was a night he will never forget.

Tom Hassell: *Tackling Bo Jackson head-to-head was the biggest thrill! Then afterwards, you see it on television, and you're like—this man was a two-sport human phenom. I'm out there and I tackled him one-on-one. That would probably be one of my biggest memories of my senior year. You had "Big Train," "Little Train," and as the announcers down in New Orleans say, "Bo-o-o-o Jackson!" I mean, oh my gosh! And we're trying to defend this? And we did! We did a great job!*

They had only three field goals. Gary Moeller told us, "You guys have to get to the ball." I didn't play for too many defense coordinators, but Gary Moeller was the most creative guy I've ever played for. He had a defense for every offense out there. And it was—it was a variation of the Michigan defense. But if there were running backs like Bo Jackson, Little Train, and

Big Train out there, Gary Moeller had an answer for it. And we did a great job against them! I credit everything to Gary because we didn't have a lot of great athletes.

Another amazing game came in 1981. I call it "the 70-Point Illinois Route." The Illini were visiting Ann Arbor and jumped out to an incredible 21-7 lead in the first quarter and were threatening to make it 28-7 when Illini quarterback Tony Eason threw an interception. From that point, Michigan scored 63 unanswered points to win it, going away 70-21. It was a huge comeback win, but the backstory to the game may be just as interesting. We get that backstory from Wolverine tight end Craig Dunaway, who was there on the field for it all.

Craig Dunaway: *That week in practice, Gary Moeller, of course, was on the staff. It was a second year, I think, and he was offensive coordinator in his second year back from Illinois. I know Bo was pissed as hell at Illinois for not givin' Mo more of a chance.*

And I know, going into that game, we really wanted to show Illinois a thing or two, and Moeller had noticed something on film about their defense. When they got into this one coverage, it was like a man-to-man defense with an outside rush, and they tipped it off with some particular alignment. So, we put in a play just for that—for that. If we saw that defense, an audible that we would go to. And—and sure enough, right before the half, I think we were up 35-21 already—or something like that—and they are in that defense. And the audible on that play would be for the receivers to do out routes, the backs to the split, and then flare out to their respective flats. And the tight ends just to run to the flat. Basically, to take all the defenders to the sideline, because they were going to have a split rush coming up the outside, and they would leave the middle wide open for a quarterback draw.

And so, Steve Smith was our quarterback, and he saw the defense and called the audible. We run that draw, and I think he's 20 yards downfield before anybody on the Illinois defense knows what's going on! The crowd noise was amazing because you're running along, and you can almost hear like this gasp.

And it was great because, to me, that was fun, particularly for Gary Moeller from his perspective. You know, it was something he had spotted. A play he had designed and put in just for this, and it was against the team that had really, we felt, had done him wrong. To me, it was a little bit of sweet revenge.

One of the most famous games in Michigan history has a simple name—the Snow Bowl. The year was 1950, November 25th; the opponent was Ohio State. The temperature was 10 degrees, and it had been blowing and snowing all night long. Reports had people at Ohio Stadium building bonfires in the stands to stay warm, and a reported 50,535 fans were on hand, although that number is disputed as too high.

How bad was it? Well, Michigan did not get a first down, they did not complete a pass, and they punted 24 times. The Buckeyes did not fare much better; they had just three first downs and punted 21 times. The most important statistic was the score and on that one, Michigan prevailed 9-3. Michigan blocked 2 punts—one for a safety and one for a touchdown—and that was the story of the Snow Bowl. But it is a game of legend, and Michigan Linebacker Roger Zatkoff, a legend himself, was right in the middle of the Snow Bowl story as a young player. It was a day he remembers very well.

Roger Zatkoff: *In those days, we took the bus from Ann Arbor to Toledo, spent the night in Toledo before the game because Ohio State hasn't changed in all these years—stuff like shutting off the water. So, we stayed in Toledo, got on a train in Toledo in the morning, and of course, in those days, the trains parked on the tracks that were right near the stadium, and we could watch people going into the stadium. As we got taped on the train with Jim Hunt, our trainer, we're sitting there waiting, because the game was delayed. We were watching people coming into the stadium, and there was one spot... it was icy, snowy, blowing over, and people would* *come down this path, hit that ice spot, and fall, which was really quite dangerous. You know, the guys are in there waiting for the next one to come and slip. So—obviously giggling—while we're sitting on the train before the game, waiting for the tarp to be shoveled off so they can get the tarp off the field, our coaches would come into our car and raise hell, and try to tell us to get our mindset on the game. Then he'd go out into another car. We'd sit there and giggle and some more—at people coming along. In hindsight, I think people should have been more concerned about people slipping on the ice but, you know, we're just a bunch of kids sitting, watching people fall on their way to the stadium.*

As we progressed to the game with just the punting contest, with Carl Kreager snapping the ball and Tony Momsen blocking and recovering a fumble, and then Ortmann, of course, doing the punting—we ended up winning that game. And I didn't play in that game because of the knee; I handed out hand warmers to the guys as they came on and off the field, always managing to keep one. That was really something, that particular game, because it really snowed, almost nobody in the stands. The people went in there and sat where they please, and it was delayed an hour and a half. And, more importantly, Northwestern had to upset Illinois in order for us to go to the Bowl. So, it was two teams upsetting one another, that caused us to get into the Rose Bowl that year.

Some games have significance as a turning point in a season, or a game can lead to a realization of just how special a team or a season can be. Such was the case back in the National Champion year of 1997. Michigan travels to Penn State. The Nittany Lions are ranked second in the nation, the Wolverines 4th. What transpired over the next 3 hours was a transformation of the Michigan team. They crushed Penn State 34-8. The Wolverine defense allowed Penn State just 169 yards of total offense. The Michigan offense rolled up a 34-0 lead into the fourth quarter. Penn State scored a meaningless TD late in the game. It was the worst home loss in the Joe Paterno era. It catapulted Michigan into the National Title conversation.

The seeds for this dominant performance came earlier in the week from a very smart coach who could motivate with the best of them. 1997 team captain Jon Jansen told me about the Penn State week and Head Coach Lloyd Carr's brilliant tactic on getting his guys ready.

Jon Jansen: *It was the most dominating performance I've ever been a part of as a football player, as a broadcaster, whatever. That game was over when Glen Steele broke through on play one and sacked their quarterback—it was over! And you know, Coach Carr had such a great part in that win. I like to tell this story because it gives you the idea of the relationship between the players and the coaches, and the fun that we had playing the game of football. I don't think that you can be a successful team if you don't have fun.*

We played Saturday and we'd have Monday off. On Sundays, we'd meet and go over the scouting report for the next game. So, when we'd go through the scouting report on Sunday, Coach Carr would always pick out one or two guys, and he would say, "Men, we're gonna go through the scouting report. You know, I called up Joe Paterno. I told him, 'Our guys, LeVar Arrington, Courtney Brown, they are some really good players. I'll give you Glen Steele. I'll give you Sam Sword. I tell you what, I'll give you our whole linebacking room just for one of those players. And it doesn't have to be both, just give me either LeVar Arrington or Courtney Brown.' You know what JoePa said? He said, 'No! Your guys aren't worth it.'"

So, you're thinking, why would coach Carr do that? He did it every week, and you wanted to be the guy that that nobody would trade for—because Lloyd mentioned your name—it was important to that player. And it was the same with Wisconsin. Coach Carr would say, "I'll give you a whole offensive line, if I can just have your backup tackle." We don't even know what this guy's name is. Barry Alvarez said, "No deal!" And so that week against Penn State, obviously it was Glen Steele.

Then Glen breaks through on the opening play of the game, sacks the quarterback, and the game is over. I really believe that, that little bit, was a great motivator for all of us. It was—it was so much fun. It just gives you kind of an insight into how in-touch Coach Carr was with the players.

A game I also love to remember is what I call, "Bo's First Bowl Win." Coach Schembechler did not have great success in his bowl career, but when he did win his first, it was a landmark game. It came in the granddaddy of them all, the Rose Bowl. After 7 tries and 7 losses, Bo and his team entered the 1981 Rose bowl against Washington, determined to get the job done. While Bo tried to downplay his record heading into the game, the media kept making it a story.

In the game, Michigan had built up a nice lead, but the Huskies defense was formidable, and it was tough sledding. At one point in the second half—and Michigan was holding on—the Wolverines were faced with a third, and very long. It was a critical call in the game, and Bo was getting all kinds of input what to do in the sideline in this tight spot. According to Rose Bowl MVP Butch Woolfolk, Bo stayed true to himself despite all the pressure and made a call that helped Michigan to a 23-6 win.

Butch Woolfolk: *It was a bold call on Bo's part; it was pretty amazing. We had, like, third down and 24, and we had Anthony Carter split out wide. Of course, the defense is looking at Anthony Carter, so they dropped back immediately. And we called a draw play…where the hell did they get that from? We called a draw play! In the huddle when they called the play, everyone was upset about it, but it opened up wide. And, of course, I just use my speed to get the first down.*

It was—it was an exciting win for him. No one was thinking about the win as much as they were thinking about it being Bo's first win, and we carried him off the field. It was great! To this day, I think that was my number one Michigan memory.

Another historic game in the modern era was the 1978 Michigan-Notre Dame game. For the first time since the 1940's these two college football powerhouses would meet again. So close geographically, it seemed like a natural. But, for different reasons, the game just didn't happen until what was called "The Reunion Game" in 1978. Can you imagine the hype? It had started when the game was scheduled by Don Canham in the late 60's, so when the date actually arrived, the college football world couldn't wait. For Michigan starting quarterback Rick Leach, the pressure of the game came from all sides.

Rick Leach: *That game probably means as much, in a lot of ways as an Ohio State game, because it was somewhere between 30 to 35 years—I think it was 32—the last time that Michigan had played Notre Dame. And the guy that I was tremendously close with, and I considered him a great friend, Bob Ufer, had talked about that game probably for two years. He always emphasized what it was going to mean, and how it was going to affect the university. He stressed to me over and over, "You're gonna play a 60-minute game, but you're gonna remember this for a lifetime. And you're gonna have to be the guy to set the tone for all the teams going forward."*

There was so much hype about the game because they had Montana and Vegas Ferguson and Jerome Heavens in the backfield. We had Huckleby and Russell Davis. There was tremendous anticipation, especially having to go down to South Bend. Now, add to the mix, I got my ankle roll up on in a Monday practice in sweats, and it ballooned up on me. And it was questionable, how effective and whether I was going to be able to play going into the game. I always knew in my heart, I didn't care what they had to do, I was playing.

And we had a rough first half—I think we were only down 14 to 7. I didn't play well; I was very inconsistent. I hadn't practiced the whole week, which was kept quiet pretty much from everybody, and I was not very effective. Now, after Schembechler got me in his office at halftime—with the door open so the whole team could hear him—he let me know, in his own special way, about what a mistake it was to even play me. I couldn't answer the bell and I'd let the whole team down…with a few other choice words. I'll never forget that, because when I walked out of there, I mean,

I had smoke coming out of my ears. He knew exactly what he was doing. He left the door open so the whole team heard it. I'll never forget when I came out of there after he had let me have it pretty good, almost to a man, I had guys come up to me and say, "Don't worry about that SOB. We're gonna go out there, we're gonna kick their ass, and we're gonna come out of here with a great victory. And you've done this, and you've done that, and we're all behind you."

And we had a great second half, things went well. We scored four touchdowns and beat them 28 to 14. I threw for three touchdowns and ran for one. And so, every kid's dream, you know, that you think about as a kid, came true for me in that game.

And after the game, Bo put his arm around me and said, "That was one hell of a performance, kid. You really stepped it up." I'm looking at him, and I'm almost in tears with a happiness, anyway, but you almost want to say, "You know, about an hour ago, you weren't too happy with me, Coach." But we've all been there with Bo. That's part of his magic as a coach, him knowing what buttons to push for everybody.

One of the most incredible games ever at Michigan Stadium was the game the great Ron Johnson had in 1968. Against Wisconsin, on a muddy field, Johnson ran for a record 347 yards and 5 touchdowns. The yardage he gained remains a record to this day, but Ron Johnson's legacy at Michigan was more than just this game. He was the consummate leader who was voted the first ever African American captain on a Michigan team.

About this iconic game, you might expect a player to remember a certain run, a particular touchdown—but, no, that isn't Ron Johnson. What Johnson remembers about this performance is its effect on others.

Ron Johnson: *Number one, Robin Fleming, who was President of the University at that time, invited my parents to come sit in his box— you know, my father, who had a fourth-grade education, my mother, who had a tenth-grade education—and, you know, in my time at Michigan,* *my parents attended every game. It was wonderful for them to be in that environment. You know, we were just all so proud of each other, and they were just so overwhelmed with what happened. They were up in a box, and then for me to have the game that I did, you got past presidents and all these people with eight zillion different degrees coming up and wanting to shake my father's hand and my mother's hand. I felt so good for them, having that pride and that experience. And I mean, that—that could not have worked out better.*

One thing that I remember is in my sophomore year, I got a varsity letter. I always felt that, as a second team player—see, I played behind Carl Ward, and Jim Detweiler, which wasn't bad stuff—but I remember we were leading Minnesota in our homecoming game my sophomore year, and it was 35 to nothing, and we didn't get in until the fourth quarter. So, my last play in the Wisconsin game was the first play of the fourth quarter. I went to Assistant Coach Tony Mason, and told Tony to put Lance Scheffler into the game, because he played behind me and l wanted the kid to get some experience, to have some fun. One of the statisticians came down about five minutes later, and said, "Ron, how many yards do you think you have?" I said, "It's probably 200." And he said, "You got 347 yards!" And my mouth just dropped!

I guess the point I'm trying to make…I could have gained over 400 yards that day with what was going on there if we wanted to run up the score and do all that other stuff. I was just taken aback; I had no clue that I had that many yards. It was just one of those magical days where, I mean, the blocking was all just so crisp, and everything else. The holes were very defined and very easy to find. It was one of those days. I was just dumbfounded; the whole day just blew me away!

In my own opinion, the most important game in the first 100 years of Michigan football was a game I participated in. I simply call it "the '69 Game" It was the Michigan-Ohio State battle of 1969. It is arguable that there are other games that rival this one, but from a selfish perspective, this game tops the list. The reason is that this game led Michigan football into an era of football excellence that is still ongoing in Ann Arbor. This Michigan victory set the stage for at least two generations of championship play and probably more.

Remember the time—1969, Bo Schembechler's first year—nobody knew who he was, and Michigan wasn't on the national map at the time. Ohio State, on the other hand, were the bullies of college football. They had not lost a game in two years. They were the defending national champs, and a shoo-in to win their 2nd in a row under the iconic Woody Hayes. The 24-12 Wolverine win would shock the college football world; It would shake the entire Big Ten Conference into a new order. It began an era when rules were changed, and traditions revised to accommodate these two larger-than-life programs and coaches. Important? In my judgement, that's an understatement.

The genesis of this seismic game actually occurred a year before in Columbus. In 1968, Michigan got blasted by Ohio State 50-14 in Ohio Stadium. At the end of that game, the Buckeyes scored a meaningless touchdown and Woody Hayes attempted a two-point conversion to run up the score and rub it in on his hated rival. It happened to be the last game the immensely respected Bump Elliott would coach at Michigan, and the last game the immensely popular and talented running back Ron Johnson would play for the Maize and Blue.

Every underclassman, and everyone on the Michigan party, were disgusted by Hayes' behavior, and the beginning of the 1969 upset was born in that devastated Michigan locker room. Ron Johnson recalls the scene.

> **Ron Johnson**: *We were all crying; we couldn't believe the '68 game. They beat us 50 to 14, and the game was so much closer than that. It was 21-14 at the half, and I remember I caught a pass in the endzone, and I was out of bounds by two inches—that would have given us a score. A ball went off Billy Harris' hands and they got it for an interception, and that sort of stuff…it just kept compounding. We*

could have won that football game, with a couple breaks, and then to have Woody to do that. And for that to be our last game. The juniors just all came over and said, "We're gonna kick their ass next year. They will pay for this. Just don't worry about it, we will take care of all this." It was just a really, really compelling thing. I remember the next year, hearing the score—I was in Cleveland for a game as a pro—and I just laughed, and laughed, and laughed. I'm just so proud of those guys! Just unbelievable.

The underclassmen made a promise to Johnson and in his first year as head coach, Schembechler understood the importance of the Ohio State game. He understood it so well that he started getting ready for the Buckeyes from the moment he stepped on campus.

Bo Schembechler*: Our defense was designed to stop the Ohio State power attack with their great fullback. We ran an offense that was similar to theirs, so that our defense could see it a lot, and learn how to defense it. Nobody else in this league had a clue, initially, how to stop Ohio State. So, we geared everything with that in mind.*

Skip forward to November of 1969. Bo Schembechler is in his first year as Michigan's coach. He's got his team playing great football. The week before we meet Ohio State, we crushed a very good Iowa team at Kinnick Stadium in Iowa. As we entered the locker room at Iowa City we were chanting, "We want Ohio State! We want Ohio State!" We may have been the only team in the country that wanted to play them and some of the coaches, including long-time assistant Jerry Hanlon went to Bo, and asked him to calm the team down—there was a concern that we might peak to early. Hanlon remembers Bo's response.

Jerry Hanlon*: It's true, because I said, "Bo, they were getting too high too soon! Look, they're all starting to talk Ohio State," and he said, "You can't get too high for Ohio State." That stuck with me. I don't guess you can, if you can back it up.*

The day of the Ohio State game was cold and wintry but as a team, we were so ready to play. None of us thought we were going to lose. As 17-point underdogs, we laughed at how stupid that seemed to us. We were just kids. I guess we didn't know any better, but we felt an incredible sense of emotion as we marched down the tunnel to the opening kick-off. My teammate, Reggie McKenzie, will never forget his experience in the tunnel that momentous day.

Reggie McKenzie: *Freshmen couldn't play, and we had a new coach. His name was Bo Schembechler, and he just beat our ass psychologically. And it took a whole bunch for me—and I'll tell you, my family really helped me getting through that—and it didn't really hit me until Ohio State. I'm coming out of that tunnel, it's Ohio State, '69, and our captain, Jim Mandich, is standing there at the top of the tunnel. I get emotional now talking about—I get emotional because I can see Mandich crying. And I realized…that's what Michigan was all about! I didn't understand it, I really didn't, until it all came on to me; there is Jim Mandich standing at the top of the tunnel, and he had tears coming down his face.*

And those guys from Ohio State, as we looked down on them—I don't know how I happen to be up front—but as we looked down at them, and they looked back at us, and they knew they had an ass whooping coming. I'll never forget it. I tell people all the time, and I get emotional every time I tell it. Because I didn't realize it, at that time, because I think I'm this big, tough kid out of Highland Park. But, watching Mandich made me understand something. I now knew exactly—I mean, he got me to where I finally realized where you had to get to, to play the game.

At that particular point in time, I grew up! I had to see it with my own eyes. And I saw it from a guy, Jim Mandich, and I told him this before— and he remembered, he said, because he was so pumped. Everybody was so pumped. Honestly, that was the greatest game I've ever participated in. You know, a lot of great things have happened to me. God's being very good to me, and the most important thing is Michigan.

Even a veteran like Hanlon, who knew what we were up against, was confident heading into the game, because this team had convinced him they could defy the odds.

> **Jerry Hanlon**: *I felt we could beat them, I really did! I really had confidence in that group of kids at that particular time. Now, "When did I know we were going to beat them?" Or, "Did I think we were going to beat them?" were two different things! I thought we could beat them. I knew at about four minutes to go in the game, when I came down out of the press box. The only time in the history of my coaching that I ever came out of the press box to be on the field at the end of the game, was that game! Because I wanted to be a part of that celebration. That was something so special that I had to be down there.*

The game itself was dominated by a little-known defensive back named Barry Pierson from St. Ignace, Michigan. With All-Americans and future Hall of Famers scattered all over the field for both sides that day, the best player in Michigan Stadium, who was head and shoulders above everybody else, was Barry.

He intercepted three Ohio State passes and returned two punts that led to scores in the 24-12 win. For Barry, he talks as if it was just another day in the office. He deflected his performance that afternoon by talking more about his teammates and his mistakes, rather than the game of his life.

> **Barry Pierson**: *What I did was my job, and if you go through that film with a fine-tooth comb, you're gonna see an awful lot of guys doing things right in order to beat Ohio State that year. I mean, there were some great plays, offensively and defensively—and special teams, of course. So, you know, it wasn't—wasn't an unusual thing, in my estimation. It was just good timing.*
>
> *I'll tell you exactly what I could have had; they're always going for the perfect scenario, right? Well, (Tom) Curtis, he stole an interception from me, and I dropped two others on down and out dives. That adds up to six*

that I could have had, so I was only 50% for the day. How's that sound? You know, you can say, "Bo did this," and "Bo's done that," and so on and so forth, but there's no way that we were ever going to lose that game, and Bo told us that from day one. He showed us how we were going to win the game, and that's exactly how we did win it. I give most of the credit to him and his staff because they had that thing figured out perfectly.

If you are a Michigan football fan and a student of its history, you know just how huge this victory was in the timeline of Wolverine Football. If you doubt me, or anyone else, about this claim, just listen to Bo Schembechler himself on the impact of this particular game.

Bo Schembechler: *Nobody knew who we were, or what we were doing. Now, don't get me wrong, they knew Michigan—it isn't like that's what put Michigan on the map—but it certainly put our program on the map, because there weren't too many people out there that knew anything about Schembechler. That wasn't exactly a household word. By beating— and you've got to get the whole picture completely, there were people saying this Ohio State team was the greatest collegiate football team of all time! Now, we're talking all time! That's what they said! It was suggested that the only team that could possibly give them a game, at that time, was the Minnesota Vikings, and apparently, they must have been the hot shots in the NFL at that time. Wasn't that the way it was?*

And so, by beating Ohio State, I mean this was unheard of! And I'm sure as that—as that game got underway and word started to spread around the country in the various stadiums that Michigan is on top of Ohio State... and then, as it came to the fourth quarter, and as you saw in the stadium, when the people were chanting and counting down, that this was a special game; this wasn't just an ordinary game. This was a magnificent upset!

And I think if you want to put it in perspective, you would have to read a letter that Fritz Crisler wrote me as he watched the game from his hospital bed. He wrote how proud he was that he was Michigan, and how Michigan stood out that day and once again expressed their dominance in college football.

PART SIX

BO STORIES,
AND STAFF STORIES

There is a dynamic that never fails whenever I'm out and amongst Michigan football fans. Whether it's as a speaker for an alumni group or just living life out in public, I invariably get the question: "Got any good Bo stories?" The answer is simple. "Of course, I do!" I've got a million of them! And so do many others who came in contact with or knew Glenn E. Bo Schembechler.

There may not be another coach in the modern era that has been as colorful or as engaging as Coach Schembechler. Because of his win-loss record, because of his demeanor, because of his passion, he became a bigger-than-life personality and the kind of guy everyone wanted their picture with. He was approachable and had a playful personality. He was all business. And at the same time, he enjoyed life and laughed as loud as the next guy when it was time for levity. As a coach, he was a disciplinarian. He made no excuses and expected none in return. You did it his way, or you didn't get a chance to do it ever again.

As a player for him, Bo stories became legendary. So, of course we've got Bo stories! This collection would not be complete without Bo stories. And we've got the young men who experienced them and lived to tell them, like running back Harlan Huckleby who, as a true freshman, lived the first of many "Bo Moments."

Harlan Huckleby: *I was a true freshman, and we were beating somebody, and so I get in the game…you know how it is when you're a freshman, you're just hyped up. I mean, you know, the big stadium, the fans, you're finally out there on the carpet. And if you got a chance, you know, so there's a bunch of us in there.*

I guess one guy probably jumps offsides. Okay, five yards. Okay, next play, somebody's holding. But we go back another 15—whatever it was—and I think I jumped the next play or something. So, we're way back. I mean, it was like third, and no way. Obviously, back then, we didn't have a pass play. It's a running play. So, we finally pull a play off. We come down the line on the option. It's on our sideline, too. And Rick pitches out, I catch it right up the chute, it's just perfect!

I'm going, I must have picked up about 20 or 30 yards but—I don't know what came over me, but here's a couple guys that come at me from the side, and I do the little Joe Washington and skip out of bounds. I don't lower the shoulder; I just do a little skip out of bounds. I had a nice run, feel pretty good, you know, I turned on the little jets and I'm feeling pretty good about myself. I skip out of bounds. I was just short of the first down! So, I'm walking down the sideline, and I see, like, people getting out of my way, so I'm thinking, "Hey, you know, I'm big stuff here!" But what it is, is Bo is coming at me—charging!

Now, the game is over, we've won it; we're well ahead. But his freshman running back, who thinks he's a bigtime freshman running back, just broke a big run and stepped out of bounds right before the first down marker. Oh, man, Bo is in my face like you would not believe! Just to make a long story short, I don't ever think—I mean even including my professional career—I don't ever think I stepped out of bounds ever again. Practice, whatever, nothing. He got it through to me. I mean, really, I'm serious! 'Til the last carry of my professional career, never did I ever step out of bounds again. But, you know, I was used to seeing, like I said, Joe Washington, guys at Oklahoma, you know, just skip out of bounds. No, not me, after Bo got a hold of me that day. I never forgot it.

Huckleby wasn't the only freshman who experienced the wrath of Bo after making a play. Defensive end Tom Seabron had a similar fate.

Tom Seabron: *It was the first game I played in, I had come there thinking I was a tight end, only to be moved to defensive end, which was fine. And it was against Northwestern. The score was 62 to nothing. The quarterback, at that particular time, is running an option that, as I went in, I was doing the cat and mouse. And when I leaped to the quarterback as he was pitching the ball, his hand in my hand met the ball together and rather than just tackle him, I grabbed the ball, spun off, and then ran, you know, 40 or 50 yards for a touchdown. If I was in today's era, I could go pro and get picked in the first round of the NFL draft now.*

But during the play, as I was running, I held a ball over my head at the 10-yard line and ran into the endzone with the ball above my head. So, Bo went absolutely crazy. So, that Sunday morning, you know, he was yelling at me for putting the ball up and running in from the 20-yard line. He just proceeded to yell, "How could you hold the ball up from the 20? We don't do that at Michigan!"

So, obviously, he was embarrassed because that made the score 69 to nothing against Northwestern. And he just—he just ripped me to shreds, and I thought I'd done something well. I think that began to set the tone, as a freshman, what this four-year experience was gonna be like. There was no such thing as adulation or gloating, because in his mind, he was the perfectionist, and he was going to always drive you to be the perfect player or the best player you could be.

While Bo could be a tyrant and admonish a player for a transgression so that player never forgot it, don't ever think Bo did not care deeply about the welfare of his guys. John Wangler tells the story about Bo being very hesitant about putting Wangler into a game following a very difficult knee injury and surgery. Wangs saw a side of Bo most never got a chance to see.

John Wangler*: Bo was a little reluctant on my knee to put me in and then finally said, "Hey, I am gonna put you in Notre Dame." It was the second game, and then I played the rest of the year. And I felt good about it, you know. It was nice to see, you know, how everyone thinks college football, at that level, is such a meat market. And Bo really was genuinely concerned about, you know, my knee, and he just was like, "Hey, are you sure? Are you sure?" I just was saying, "C'mon, Bo, just let me play! I'm fine, I'm fine!" I had all the clearance and everything, but it was like your dad. You know, a lot of people didn't see that side of the compassion that Bo had for everybody. I remember him calling all the linemen together before he put me back in against Notre Dame and he said, "I don't want them laying a hand on him!" And so, I mean, that stuff was special, you know, little stuff like that.*

The late Vada Murray, one of Bo's finest safeties, remembers a Bo story that had nothing to do with football; it was all about how to handle yourself off the football field.

Vada Murray*: One memory that I had at Michigan wasn't even football related. We're at the Rose Bowl, and Bob Hope had that party for us. And, I can remember, a lot of players took their sport coats off at the dinner table. The next day of practice, that's all Bo could talk about, was how inappropriate that was and how, you know, in the business world, when you get out of college, you don't do that. Right then and there, that told me, as far as being at Michigan, football was secondary. He was getting us ready for life.*

Many Bo stories come from players who were called into Bo's office. You probably should know that getting called into Bo's office was *not* one of your most favorite things when you were a player. In some cases, before you went into Bo's office, you checked in at St. Mary's student chapel for the last rites from the pastor.

Just kidding! Anyway, one of the greatest "Getting Called into Bo's Office" stories comes from linebacker and team captain Andy Cannavino.

Andy Cannavino*: We had lost our last three games of the year to Purdue, to Ohio State, and then to North Carolina in the Gator Bowl. So, we finished my junior year 0-3. We start my senior year one and two, and the only victory was against Northwestern 17 to 14, and I actually intercepted a pass in the endzone. They were on our 20-yard line going in to score and tie the game with a minute to go. So, we were actually— we were one and five in our last six games. And everyone was asking, "What's wrong, what's going on?" Blah, blah, blah. And because we were a young team—especially on defense—my senior year, we were doing a lot of hitting during practice, which is not as common as most teams, and doing a lot of things like that.*

So, to make a long story short, at the same time, Ohio State had hired Earl Bruce year before. And they went 11-1 our junior year, and they were 3-0 my senior, and they kept talking in the papers, how much fun they're having under Earl, and doing all these wonderful things under Earl that they weren't doing under Woody. So, I just mentioned it casually to Bill McCartney, our defensive coordinator, and Mac asked, you know, "What's going on?" I said, "Well, you know, we're just not having any fun, and everybody's working so hard, and everybody's bummed out, and we're not winning. And when you're not winning, no one's having any fun. And guys are all grumbling about how long the practices are," and blah, blah, blah. And back then—I'm sure you guys had the same thing—we had very good relationships with the coaches. We'd call them by their first names and all that. So, when Mac asked me, it was just like talking to a friend, you know.

Well, the next morning, like at seven in the morning, I get a phone call at my house. It's Bo's secretary and she says, "Bo wants to see you." And I go, "Wow, you know, I don't know what he would want in middle the season." So, I get dressed and go there about 8:30 in the morning. You know, Bo's secretary greets me, and I walk in, and Bo opens the door, and as soon as he closes it he just starts screaming at me. And I sit down, and he sits behind his desk, and he's actually, literally, physically reaching over his desk, "How dare you tell us we're working too hard?

You're my captain!" And he's spitting and screaming and yelling, and I was kind of taken aback because the comment I'd made to McCartney a few days earlier, I didn't really take it all that seriously; it was a 30 second conversation. It wasn't like I sat down for an hour to explain everything that was wrong with Michigan football. So, he just started screaming, "You're my captain, and you gotta be me on the field! Who do you think you are? And you want me to call Reggie McKenzie and Dan Dierdorf, and these guys, and tell them that you're working too hard?" and blah, blah, blah." And he just went off and he went crazy. And I swear to God, I sat there and I started crying. Tears were in my eyes. And I didn't know what to say, because I literally—number one—I didn't think I really had said anything that bad. And he just went off and went crazy. He went off for like, five, eight, ten minutes. I mean, it seemed like an eternity. And he just flipping out on me screaming and yelling, "You know, you gotta be me on the field!" and, "Who do you think you are?" And, you know, "I should call up all these old players and these guys and ask them if they were tired."

And then, at the end of the conversation, I'll never forget what he did say, which I thought was interesting. He said, "You're gonna leave this room today, and you are going to be me on the field. You're going to become my greatest captain ever. And we are going to win every single game from here on in, and the Rose Bowl!" And I swear to God, he said that, I laughed, and I swear to God on the Bible, I actually did change a lot.

I became more vocal on the field, I gave more orders, and I really did become a good captain, I really believe that. And we ended up winning every game, and luckily, because of that, and because we won Bo's first Rose Bowl, kind of got the monkey off his back. He, you know, he tells people, and that story about how I became his greatest captain—a lot of it was luck, of course. A lot of it's being in the right place at the right time. And of course, you know, if we don't win every game, the story never becomes told. "

The story does get told though, because it's true. Andy may downplay it, but the reality is that it was a turning point in his life and a turning point for that football team. Years after the meeting in his office. Bo still remembered the emotional session and the lesson both learned in that season.

Bo Schembechler*: I went after Andy hard. I asked him if he'd heard any of those things. He said he had. I said, "Did you ever say any of them yourself?" And he said, "Yes, I did." I got a little upset, because Andy's father played at Ohio State. Ohio State hadn't offered this young man a grant-in-aid. We brought him to Michigan, made him an all-Big Ten linebacker. His teammates elected him captain of the team, and it ends up the that he's one of our problems here as far as attitude is concerned. So, I went after him hard. When it was over, Andy got up, and he had tears coming down his cheeks, because I really went after him. He went out the door, and from that point on, in my judgment, Andy Cannavino was the greatest captain I've ever had at Michigan. He was unbelievable in practice. He led a defensive team—I think it was, like, 21 consecutive quarters—nobody crossed our goal line. We beat everybody, we beat them all! We were so enthusiastic. And when we played, the enthusiasm just permeated throughout the squad and—and people that watched us knew that this was a squad that was together with a purpose.*

We won the Rose Bowl. At the end of the season, in my opinion, that was the greatest football team in the United States of America. We didn't win the National Championship because the head coach made one classic mistake; he didn't coach attitude, like you should. Anybody who's going to coach today had better coach attitude every single day of the week with every player he's got, and not take for granted if someone's elected captain, they know what to do as captain. You bring the captain in and you sit him down and you tell him how important his responsibilities are, that he's the coach on and off the field, that he represents me. That the players look to him, and that he's got to be the right kind of a guy. Cannavino was a sensational player, and ended up being a great, great captain.

Bo never played favorites, either. If you violated one of the standards Bo had set, you paid the price. As a sophomore at spring practice, I watched as Bo banished Barry Pearson and Jim Mandich, both All-Americans, from practice for getting into a post-play skirmish. I'm thinking, "Wait a minute, these are two of our best! What's Bo doing?" What he was doing was making a point. And as far as Barry Pearson was concerned, it was all a matter of protecting your territory.

Barry Pearson: *Really, I was trying to earn a position, you know, and I wasn't foolin' around. So, I'd come in there, no matter what, and make a hit. And a lot of times, I'd hit late, you know, and Mandich figured I hit late, so he came up and threw a knee into me, and we just went at it. And Bo said, "That's enough of that, you guys are out of here!" So, lo and behold, we went and shot pool at the Union. Yeah, there was blood out there, but we were pretty much friends, I thought. Well, you got to understand the—I would come in there and hit somebody, and of course, Bo would yell, because he's the offensive coach, right? Well, then Dick Hunter would tell me to do it again. He'd say, "Do it again." So, you know, those guys had it going, too. That's pretty much what was going on. It was no big deal! Nobody was worried about it, I don't think. It was kind of funny, yeah, we're going off with our heads between our tails.*

Maybe the guy who got away with the most with Coach Schembechler was Jim Betts. Jim was an exceptional athlete who, as a junior, was playing quarterback, and behind Don Morehead on the depth chart. Betts was too good to sit on the bench, and he could play elsewhere and be a major contributor, and he knew it. So, Rope, as we called Betts, decided he needed to see Bo and get his position changed so he could see more playing time.

Jim Betts: *I went to him because, you know, looking at the way things were. Barry (Pearson) was gone, (Tom) Curtis, was gone, Healy was gone. So, the only guy coming back was Darden, you know, and I'm not gonna sit on this pine another year. And so, I'm gonna go over to play defense. And so, I talked to Hunter first and I said, "You know, I want to come over and play safety," and he said, "Bring your ass over!" I went to*

Bo and I said, "Bo, I'm moving over to defense, play safety." He said, "I'll be a son of a bitch, you don't walk in here and tell me what you're gonna do. Dammit, you're my quarterback!" I said, "No, Moorehead is your quarterback. I back him up." He said, "Well, same damn difference." I said, "Well, look, I am not gonna sit on the bench this year. I'm gonna go play defense." He says, "I'll tell you what you're gonna do; you're gonna play both damn positions." I said, "I don't care, that's fine with me. But I'm not sitting on that bench again, I can tell you that." Bo said, "You better just be ready to go when you have to go in." I said, "Hey, anybody can go in there and hand the ball off."

(Laughter)

And then Bo said, "Get the hell outta here!"

Betts moving to safety proved to be a very smart too, as he made all Big Ten in just one year at the position.

But Rope was also one of those guys who loved to prank others. He was articulate and could charm anyone with an incredibly smooth rhetoric and vocabulary. As an African American, he was also socially conscious during a very socially conscious time in our history. Bo, of course, was a strict disciplinarian. He had definite ideas on grooming and hair length, and things of that nature, for his team that in the late 60s and early 70s, at times, became an issue. Jim Betts decided that the collision of culture should happen, and it resulted in one of the greatest Bo stories ever.

Jim Betts: *His thing was, he was letting the afros and all the rest of that hair go. But no mustaches, no goatees, no beards, and cut those sideburns down to the ear lobe. And I was saying to myself, "Man, this is really messed up. I'm just getting to where I can see my mustache, and he wants me to shave it off." I said, "Well, I ain't going for it, but I better have a pretty convincing argument."*

Yeah, I went to his office the next day, and said, "Bo, you know, I understand the whole team concept that you're espousing and how it's important that, you know, we don't have distractions that can interfere with the whole team concept." I said, "And I want to also let you know that, you know, we're willing to do anything we have to do to be winners, but you know, you stepped into an area that is pretty sensitive right about now, and that is this whole identity thing, as it relates to a black man's heritage. You've asked that we shave off our mustaches, which is basically denying who we are as people." And I said, "I really find that difficult to do at this time in my life. If you look around, you will not see a black man without a mustache. You know, there's certain things that we're able to hold on to that—that differentiates us from anybody else, and having a mustache is one of those things, and I'm telling you right now, I'm not gonna shave mine off." He looked at me and he said, "What kind of happy horseshit is that?" And I said, "I'm telling you that this is serious, and I'm as serious as a heart attack. I'm telling you—you are really asking some guys to do some things that will just go against the grain. It's gonna cause a problem. And I feel strongly about it that I'm not gonna shave my mustache. I'll do anything else, but I'm not gonna shave my mustache." And he looked at me again, and this is one of the first times I could barely keep from laughing, because normally I'd laugh through the whole damn thing. But I maintained a serious look—I should have been one of the first black men up for an Academy Award for a lead performance—and so, he looked at me and he didn't know—he just did not know if I was serious or not. So, the only thing he could do was say, "Get the hell out of my office."

The next day, when we came into Yost and we formed that little circle, and he gave us instructions, he said, "You know, I've been informed that it's a black man's heritage to have a mustache, so the black guys can keep theirs." I never thought he was gonna buy it, to be honest with you. And I was prepared to shave it off. And the only person that really thought that it came from me was Henry Hill, because he kind of looked back at me with this look on his face, and I just played dumb.

If Betts was a wordsmith, Bo was his equal when it came to getting his team ready for football games. I never knew anybody who could find the right phrase at the perfect time to motivate a group of guys to give their best. Former Wolverine safety Jeff Cohen told me Bo was the absolute best at getting a team ready to go.

Jeff Cohen: *He knew exactly what to say. And I remember we were out in Iowa one year—Jerry Diorio and Vince deFelice roomed together—and I remember them coming down the next morning, they were—they were so jacked. They said, "Man, the old man walked into our room and he looked at us and he said, '64 men versus the whole fucking state,' then he turned and walked out of the room, leaving you there ready to, like, you know, go through the wall." But, I mean, you know, those are—those are great things that you just never forget, you know.*

And then I remember going down to Columbus one year and, you know, after the team movie, and the defensive backs all had a brief meeting, and we're walking back to our room and Milan Vooletich comes walking down the hall and he stops us all. He looks at us, "You know, you guys are the luckiest sons of bitches in the world." "So, why is that, Milo?" He said, "Because you could have come here and gone to school and been an asshole the rest of your life." Man, you can just picture yourself there and him saying that, and getting chills.

There's no question Bo knew what buttons to push with each and every individual that came through the program. He was a master at getting the most out of anyone who came under his charge. The great Reggie McKenzie tells the story of how he almost walked away from it. Bo was just too much for him.

Reggie McKenzie: *He just talked bad to us. I'm saying, you know, "I don't have to take this." I'll never forget, it was after one ball game. We're walking up the tunnel and my mother and my sister, Jeanetta—who is not with us anymore, she's in glory—and I'm saying, "Mom, I don't know how much more I can take from this guy. I don't know whether there is something about me he don't like, and I really don't care a whole lot* *about him. So, I'm thinking about leaving." And my sister Jeanetta says, "Mackenzie's don't quit," and that was the last time in my life that I ever mentioned word "quit." And I never said it again. Because it stays in my mind, what my sister Jeanetta said when she said, "McKenzie's don't quit."*

And that was the end of our sophomore year, and then my junior year, we started playing. We learned how to beat him. It was just doing right every time, all the time, the first time, and he couldn't say anything to you.

As time went by, Bo became a very savvy media personality. Because of his success, he was in demand as a speaker, and because of his opinions, he made great copy. So, the idea came about to start a television show with Bo Schembechler as the main character. A coach's show, if you will.

Well, way back, years before, a Detroit television station had aired a college football show that featured both Michigan and Michigan State, and it was called the Bump and Duffy Show. It referred to the head coaches at both schools, Bump Elliot and Duffy Daugherty. When the idea of a similar show came up in discussions with Bo, the coach bristled at the suggested name and stood up in a meeting and blustered with great conviction, "It will be *The Bo Show*, or no show!" Bo was ready to walk out of the meeting right then and there! Is the story truth or fiction? According to show producer Bob Lipson, who was in the meeting, that's the gospel truth.

Bob Lipson*: That is a direct quote, yeah. That is a true story, and it really happened! And the feeling was, at the time he said it, that it would be no show. Then one was put together, because he wanted, I mean, he saw—this was already 1975. He had already been there for some time, and he just felt he wanted to branch out and build his program with his name only, and it was a tough name to remember.*

And there was a two-folded way of paying him. Obviously, he got paid for doing the show itself. But there was also what we created, and this came from the old days down in Alabama, with Bear Bryant. It was what they called a "crawl" at the end of the show, where you would just run a bunch of names, and these people would all pay x-amount of dollars to have their names run at the end of the show. It was kind of, like, within the credits. And that money went directly to Bo, and that's really where he made most of his money. He didn't make a lot of money as the head coach. And there were companies—and quite honestly, these were mostly companies that weren't traditional television advertising companies—so, these were not the guys that you would normally see a TV ad made from. They would be industrial companies and things like that. But they jumped in and, let's face it, they were Michigan fans, and the whole push was really to help Bo financially.

Bo was a frightening kind of a character because of his reputation. So, yeah, you had—you walked on eggs around him. I'll be honest with you, even starting the show, the first year or two, you walked on eggs a bit because he was very guarded. First of all, he never loved the media, you know that as well as anybody; he was never a media lover. And he treated me with suspicion, even though I tried to tell him, "I am not the media." And that changed after a couple of—three years, basically—that's when he knew I wasn't going to do anything to screw things up."

Despite the payment schedule and how much Bo would make from the program, it wasn't called *The Bo Show* officially. It was called *Michigan Replay* and according to Lipson, that was for a reason.

Bob Lipson: *I did it on purpose because I believed at the time, somewhere, someway, somehow, sometime down the road, Bo will not be the head coach of that television show. But I want that television show to continue whoever that next guy is. So, by calling it Michigan Replay, it allows it to be what it was. It could have a life. Now, what I didn't know at the time, was how long Bo was gonna be around, and God love him, I appreciate the fact that he was around for a long time. But that was—that was one of the reasons, and also the fact that people had a hard time with* *the name: Schembechler. In fact, I tease everybody—they asked me, how did I get the gig? And I say, "Well, I could spell Schembechler, and that's the reason." The truth was that I wanted the show to last past Bo's time, and over the years it did, because then Gary Moeller came along, and then Lloyd."*

The show *Michigan Replay* lasted for nearly 30 years and, as Lipson predicted, it stayed *Michigan Replay* through Gary Moeller and Lloyd Carr's years as coach. It morphed into *Inside Michigan Football* when Rich Rodriguez took over and is still on the air today. But back in the mid 70s, when *Michigan Replay* debuted on Channel 7 in Detroit, it didn't get off to a rip-roaring start, according to then-co-host Larry Adderley.

Larry Adderley*: We had it all planned, and everything was gonna run smoothly, and the idea was to do the show in one take, which would help the coach and all that because he was the rookie, as far as broadcasting was concerned. And the first game was at Wisconsin, so, what we had to do, was to make arrangements to get coaching tape. And in this instance, it came back—double sprocket holes on each side of the film. So, our guys loaded it and it was silent; it was just coaching film. So, we weren't gonna have crowd noise and things like that. And everything was all set, as far as we were concerned.*

We rolled the intro to the show and got it started. Didn't take us long, because that was the format, to get into the highlights of the game. And there they were, Coach started commenting on them, and I was trying to help him along to point out the highlights that we had chosen. And then came the first touchdown…and the picture of the endzone came up and there was the word Wisconsin—written backwards!

(Laughter)

All of a sudden, we knew we had something wrong, and I mentioned it and Bo said, "Yeah, I wondered why Rick was right-handed."

While Bo stories are plentiful, we're not going to forget what I call "staff stories." Members of the coaching staff over the years have had their moments, too. These men had a unique perspective on the happenings of the program. They were in the middle of the action and they were all excellent at their craft. Some of them moved on to head coaching positions themselves, but without question, they all contributed greatly to Michigan's football success.

Some of them even enjoyed poking their bosses a little bit. Back when Benny Oosterbaan was the coach, Cliff Keen, Michigan's legendary wrestling coach, was doubling up by coaching on the football staff, too. One day, Keen played a bit of a prank on his head coach Benny Oosterbaan with the help of a couple of exceptional freshmen named Ted Toper and Roger Zatkoff. I'll let Roger finish the story.

> **Roger Zatkoff**: *So, you know how Monday practice goes—the guys that don't get in on Saturday, they want to get a little workout on Monday. So, what happens is, they put a couple of tackling dummies up, and then they gave the ball to the quarterback, and he would hand the ball off to the halfback and the coach would say, "Run through the hole!" And there's Tope and I sitting there, tackling them to get them toughened up a little bit. And Tope and I would really work them over, you know, that day, and we had fun. We were just killin' em." So, the following day, Oosty sends the manager over and he says, "Send two more guys for tackling drills, and don't send Zatkoff and Toper." He tells that to Cliff Keen, and Keen looks at us and he winks, and he says, "You guys go." So, we get about halfway there, and Oosterbaan jumps up and says, "Go back, send me two more. I don't want you guys here. You're gonna kill us! We won't be able to play on Saturday."*

Some 30 years later, another assistant coach had to leave a practice to find a freshman, but it wasn't to help out in a drill; it was to get him back to practice. It is a legendary story about the great Anthony Carter. When Carter was a freshman, legend has it that Anthony was very close to leaving Michigan. There are conflicting reports about this event, but the principles in this tale are head coach Bo Schembechler, assistant coach Bob Thornbladh, and Carter. For the record, Thornbladh tells us all how it went down.

Bob Thornbladh: *Anthony showed up on campus and we expected that he would be a good player. And we took him out for the first practice and some balls were clearly overthrown, and we just turned around to walk back to huddle. All of a sudden, we heard the kids cheer. Carter had run underneath the ball—I mean he had this tremendous ability to accelerate, you know! He had a great sort of game speed, and he caught the ball. And, I'll never forget, Bo came in and said, "Men, we got something special here. We got a player, I don't think, like we've ever had. Now, we don't know how to pass or what we're doing, but this kid is special!" He wowed us at that first freshman practice. So, we were all excited about it.*

When we come back to the second practice and we have a staff meeting, we go out there and the kids are stretching, and we go out there and I'm looking around, and Anthony is not there. And Bo says to me, "Where the hell is Carter? Where the hell is Carter?" I said, "Oh my God, he's not here!" And Bo didn't say a word, because Bo would never excuse a coach from practice to go chase a player. If you don't want to come to practice and play for Michigan, that's fine—that's a privilege, and you're no longer going to be awarded that privilege. You're gone! But I said, "Coach, I'm gonna go find him."

So, I took Mike Gittleson and we went off to the dorm, hoping he'd overslept. We couldn't find him. We went to the basketball courts; we went all over. By that time, practice was over. We had searched all over, but Bo kept telling us to go find him. So, I told Coach, "We're going to the airport." So, Mike Gittleson and I went to the airport, and we searched all over the airport. There was a flight that evening leaving for Fort Lauderdale, but we still couldn't find him anywhere.

We finally found him in a video game area in the old Metro airport, which was up on the balcony. So, we said, "Anthony, you know, before you leave, Bo just wants to talk to you." And I like to tell the story that Bo said, "Tackle him!" and I missed him 10 times. So anyway, he got on the phone with Bo, and Anthony goes, "Uh huh, uh huh, uh huh. Okay," and he hung up. And I said, "Anthony, what did Bo say?" He said, "Bo said I could go home." He got on the plane, so I called Bo. I said, "Bo, he told me you told him he could leave." Bo yelled back, "I didn't tell him he could leave!"

But the gist of the story is this: we had some people meet him down there and they talked him into coming back. He was just a little homesick, he said, and he was going to come back, and he would like to know when Picture Day was so he could be back for Picture Day. That's the Anthony Carter in the airport story. The rest is football, Michigan lore, and history."

As you can tell, Bob Thornbladh is quite a character. Even as a player back in the early 70s, Bob was making memories dishing out his brand of advice to anyone who would listen. On one occasion, Bob gave a new assistant coach at Michigan a quick lesson in what Michigan football was all about. That assistant was Jack Harbaugh, and I'll let Jack pick it up from there.

Jack Harbaugh*: The first game that I ever coached here on Bo's staff was Iowa. All I could think about all year long is, "Michigan always beat Iowa and beat them badly for a lot of years, and the only difference was Jack Harbaugh." If we lost, if Michigan lost that game, it may be the last game that I ever coach at Michigan. So, I'm in the locker room, and I get sweat coming off my forehead. My palms are sweating and I'm in the locker room, and Bob Thornbladh is playing at the time; he's a fullback. So, he's putting on his uniform, and he's looking at me. Bob said, "What the hell is wrong with you?" I said, "You don't understand! If we don't win this game, this could be the last game that I ever coach." Now, he's a player, and I'm a coach. Bob Thornbladh looked at me and here's what he* *said, "Jack," this is like an hour before the kickoff and he's a player—he's only 20 years old, but he's Bob Thornbladh, and he looks at me and says, "Jack, they are Iowa…we're Michigan. We are not gonna lose, no matter who's here. We're not losing to Iowa!" That was the attitude that I finally learned, and you know, there is something to that."*

In his career at Michigan, Jack Harbaugh turned out to be a great coach. He went on to head coaching positions after his time at Michigan, and he raised two sons who turned out to be pretty darn good coaches themselves in Jim and John. But Jack's stories as an assistant coach at Michigan under Schembechler are priceless, like this one about becoming the Michigan film coach.

Jack Harbaugh*: At seven o'clock on Sunday, the film coach had to have three games in a row sitting in front of Bo in that old meeting room down there on Hoover and State. If they weren't there, I mean, I'd hear, "Harbaugh, I don't know why I brought you in here! You can't get me three game films?" That was what I was going to hear. So, that was all part of my job.*

So, how I got the job was, Elliot Uzelac and I got the job at the same time. We were hired the same day, and we're playing racquetball with Bo, and we're down in that old building after we played and Bo says, "You know, there's a film coach job open." "I don't think I want the job," and Elliott says, "I don't think I want it, either." And Bo says, "Well, one of the two of you is going to have it, so we are going to do this by flipping a coin. That's fair." So, Bo flips the coin, and asks, "Heads or tails?" I said, "Heads." It came up heads. "Jack, you got it!" he says. So, I said, "Wait a minute! I won the toss, why do I have the job?"

(Laughter)

"If I won the toss, I should have the right to say that Elliott has it, right?" Bo says, "Dammit Harbaugh, do you want to coach here or not?" So, I got the film job.

So then, the biggest problem I had was Illinois. They would send their film on Sunday morning. It had to go through Chicago, and then to Detroit. So, there's only one flight that you could get that would do that, and the flight got in here about two or three o'clock, and I knew I would have plenty time. I send a guy out to the Metro airport and he says, "Coach, no film, it's not on the plane." I say, "It's got to be on the plane, it's the only flight!" I didn't have time to put somebody in a car and drive them to Peoria or someplace to make the exchange. I figured the only chance I have is, I gotta get a hold of the Chicago airport and see if they can find it.

So, I'm calling, and on about the third call I'm finally in the loading dock of the Chicago airport. I'm talking to a guy named Joe. I say, "Joe, Jack Harbaugh. You don't know me, but I'm the secondary coach at the University of Michigan; I'm the film coach. Have you ever heard of Bo Schembechler?" He says, "I have, yeah, isn't he that guy that gets kind of wild on the sideline?" I say, "Well, he's got a little bit of a temper. And let me tell you something; I have three children: John, Jim, and Joanie. They're in sixth and seventh grade, and my job is a film coach—I have to have three games in front of him at seven o'clock or I'm gone, I'm fired. I'm gonna have to go home and tell my wife Jackie and three kids that I'm no longer gonna be coaching." I mean, I'm running this on this guy. I'm giving him the whole shot. I say, "Joe, could you just kind of look around there and see if you could find four cans of film that could be sent to Ann Arbor?" So, he comes back and he goes, "Coach Harbaugh, its Joe. I got good news for you! Give your wife Jackie a call and tell her you're still hired at the University of Michigan."

Over the years, along with Jack Harbaugh, Michigan has been blessed with some great assistant coaches. One of those great ones was Jerry Hanlon. He came to Michigan in 1969 with Bo as an offensive line coach and, in my opinion, was one of the best of all time. After that, he moved on to coach the quarterbacks and help them reach All-American status, too. Jerry Hanlon is simply a great coach with a passion for football that is unmatched, and a love for Michigan football that is unrivaled. On one occasion, Jerry took over for Bo in the pregame locker room before a huge rivalry game. His message to the team was unforgettable, and offensive guard Doug James will never forget it.

Doug James*: In 1983, George Perles had become the head coach at Michigan State, and he went out and he recruited, and he was quoted as saying, "We knocked the socks off Michigan in recruiting." It really kind of set the stage when we went to East Lansing. They were at a good team with Carl Banks and Ingram and all these great players, and Bo had always kind of made the pregame his deal, and Hanlon just kind of took over.*

And you know how Jerry is—he cries when he talks—and he got up in front of the team and he said, "Don't let any son of a bitch think he can come in here and replace what this man," and he pointed at Bo, "has done at Michigan." We were all so pumped up and fired up. And while I can't remember everything that Jerry said, it was probably the best pregame speech I've ever heard. And we roared out of the locker room and we beat those sons of bitches 42 to nothing, and I swear, if we had the ball, we'd be going in for a score right now. That was a great memory for me.

This Hanlon pregame speech must have been special because I was offered, unsolicited, another version of the event from James' teammate, Jeff Cohen. It's the same story, just from a different perspective.

Jeff Cohen*: It was George Perles's first year at Michigan State. If you remember, he came in, and he talked about how they knocked our socks off in recruiting and how their program was at the same level as ours. That really pissed us off, and I'll never forget going up there for that game in East Lansing. The night before, you know, Bo would come in and check you in, and we drove to Jackson. We stayed in Jackson and we bused up to East Lansing the morning of the game. I think it was—it was my last year. So, it was—Hewlett and I were rooming together that year—that year. And he said—he said, "Men, tomorrow we're going into battle, and I just want to know… are you with me?" And we said, "Hell yeah, we're* *with you." He said "Good! Because tomorrow, I don't care who we are out there, whether we're a bunch of Greeks, Italians, blacks, Jews, I don't care if we're purple of if we're yellow! Whatever we are, we're going out there tomorrow as one. And we're going out there as Michigan, and I just want to make sure you're with me!" You know, when a guy walks out of a room and says that, walks out of the room, you're just, like, ready to jump through the wall.*

So, we go up there, and Jerry Hanlon gave one of the greatest pregame speeches that I've ever heard where he got emotional, and you looked around that locker room, guys were crying. And he was talking about, you know, he pointed to Bo, and he said, "It's taken this man 15 years to get this program where it's at, and how dare they come in, in their first year, and claim that their program is at the same level as ours!"

And we went out, beat them 42 to nothing, and we could have scored 100 If we wanted. We had guys crying! I mean, when we went out there, you almost felt sorry for those poor bastards because we knew we're gonna kick their ass so bad!

On that occasion, Jerry Hanlon clearly took over for Bo and proved what a team effort the entire operation was. Players, head coach, and assistant coaches, all working together toward victory—that whole idea carried through at Michigan beyond the Schembechler years.

In 1997, the year of Michigan's last National Championship, Lloyd Carr needed to gather himself as a head coach and restore confidence and resolve in his team in a game against Iowa. The Wolverines had played a terrible first half and were watching their National Title hopes disappear in Michigan Stadium against the Hawkeyes. It was at halftime of that game that assistant coach Mike DeBord learned a lesson about coaching and leadership from Lloyd Carr.

Mike DeBord: *The first half, Brian Griese came out and threw a couple interceptions, and they ran a punt return against us right before the* *half. And you know—and I thought, "Lloyd is gonna go in and really get after this team. He's gonna go in there at halftime and probably attack them and the coaches, everybody else."*

*But I'll tell you what, he went in, and it was probably the best job of a halftime that I've ever seen by a coach. He went in and he got the whole team together, he got the coaches together. And he said, "Look, that wasn't us in the first half. We're only down by this amount of points." And he said, "Now, is there a man in here that doesn't believe we can come back and win this football game?" And you could just feel the energy come out of that, and everybody was saying, "Yeah! Yeah! We can win!" And he says, "'I want everybody to get their poise, get under control. And let's go back out, and let's get this thing, play by play, and let's win it!" *

And that's exactly what happened! We went out and, play by play, we got into position to win the game at the end. And I just think that was probably a masterful job of coaching that whole season. He did a great job, as well as the whole coaching staff, of keeping that team focused. Because, obviously, when the wins started adding up, and we got to get closer and closer to the end, the pressure started mounting. And he took the pressure off of all the coaches and the players and said, "Hey, let's go have fun! And let's coach and play, and let's do, you know—let's get this thing done!" And that was a lot of fun at the end, where it could have been a lot of pressure.

That game wasn't the first time that season that DeBord got a reminder from Coach Carr not to get hung up in the moment.

Mike DeBord: *That was the first season that I called the offense. And I remember in our first ball game, you know—obviously had little extra jitters because of calling the game—and I never forget, I called two passes right in a row. And all of a sudden, I heard—right in the middle of a series—I heard from Lloyd, "Hey, Mike, this is Michigan, not BYU!" And so, right then, that whole deal was set. Oh, we gotta get back to running the ball.*

Sometimes, things happen on the sideline that never get reported in the aftermath of a game. There's so much going on—little things that get lost in the big picture of the outcome of the contest. In the middle of the controlled chaos of a sideline, things happen that get lost until the game is over and you start to remember the details. One such event occurred in Wisconsin during a road game against the Badgers. It happened to assistant coach Fred Jackson, and at the time, it was no laughing matter.

Fred Jackson: *It was very, very cold. I don't know exact temperature, but I know it was as cold as you can be in a football game, and we had just had a drive stall, the kids come over to the sidelines. Chris Howard and Chris Floyd sitting in front of these big, long burners. You know, you can see fire shooting out of them a little bit, you know, but really, it's just to get your hands warm. But I had Chris Howard and Chris Floyd sitting there, and I'm trying to talk to them about what we're gonna do the next series, so I put my hands together, and was rubbing my hands in front of the burner. I look around and Chris Floyd says, "Coach, your gloves are on fire." And I looked at my hands, and the tip of my gloves was on fire! And I didn't have the time to grab the back ends of the gloves, so all I could do was stick them at Chris Floyd and Chris Howard and have them slap them out. So, that was the way I got them out. They hadn't started to burn my fingers yet, but I figured by the time I would have taken the sleeves off, I would have had a problem. That was pretty funny, and it just so happened that Stan Parrish saw it, and Stan Parrish told somebody on the phones that Fred's gloves were on fire. But the kids put the fire out, and we went on to play a decent football game and won on the road.*

Jackson is right. Assistant Coach, Stan Parrish was a witness to the fire.

Stan Parrish: *Yeah, it was just really freezing there that day, and we were number one in the nation. We're getting the ball back, and we were both down at the same end of the bench. I was getting ready to give the quarterback the play when I heard over the phone that Fred was on fire. Of course, you know, there's always a little bit of levity in football. But* *as I look back, he's exactly right. I was the—one of the first to see that he put his hands on one of those warmers, and that his gloves were singeing. In all the tension of the day and the moment, it's those kinds of things you remember forever. I'll never forget Fred saying, "My gloves are on fire back here!"*

Assistant coaches see it all during a career. It can mold them into their progression to being a head coach, or it can give them the experience to become better each and every year. For Erik Campbell, one of the great learning experiences he had was coaching Michigan's Charles Woodson. In his last season, Woodson was a three-way player. He was a cornerback on defense, a receiver on offense, and a return man on special teams. In reality, Woodson had three position coaches, but Campbell kind of got the nod as Woodson's main position coach. Charles was so talented, it was really an easy job, but Erik did have his moments with the Heisman Trophy-winner.

Erik Campbell: *We had Woodson practicing both ways, you know, during week. And I remember a couple times, we were trying to get him to play quarterback and we tried to run him on a quarterback draw, and Woodson would say, "Oh no, I hurt my knee, my knee hurt, I can't do it!" And Lloyd got so upset, he'd say to Woodson, "Get out of there, get out of there, and go back to defense." But it was fun. I mean, he came in, and he loved the game. All he wanted to know was, "what is the game plan? What do I have to do? And give me the ball!" That's all he wanted to know, and how many times he'd get it during the game. And if he didn't get it enough, he'd get upset. We'd talk about routes during the season. That summer, you know, we had to run routes, so we got him ready to run routes. All he wanted to know was, "What route am I running? and when am I getting the ball?"*

When we struggled on offense, and we needed to make a play, and his number was called, we knew the ball was going to him. And he came up with the big play. We wound up winning the game. That's right, we just

tell Woodson to go down the field and turn around and just catch the ball.
"Once you catch it, make your magic happen." And that's what he did!

Besides X's and O's, fire hazards, running down AWOL players, searching for film canisters, coaching uber talented teenagers, and keeping your head coach happy, assistant coaches, I learned, must also have one other skill—they got to keep their heads on a swivel. It can get dangerous out there! Former assistant coach Bobby Morrison learned that lesson the hard way.

Bobby Morrison: *We're on the practice field, and Mike Gittleson had just finished stretching them, and we broke the stretch. I was in the way of Jon Jansen, who turned and was sprinting to the other field, and I was standing right in his way. Needless to say, he hit me with his helmet right in the chest, knocked the wind out of me. I thought I was close to dead. But I came back and coached hard, and was all right.*

So, about two weeks later, or three weeks later, we're playing Wisconsin. And I'm coaching the special teams and Wisconsin had punted the ball, and we were jamming their gunner. I put two guys out there on their gunner. And so, we're jamming the gunner and I was watching the ball as the ball came down the field on the sidelines, and I'm moving down, and I'm moving down, and we're kicking the hell out of this gunner—we even knock him out of bounds! Well, the guy is still running, but he's out of bounds, and he hits me hard, and the doctors were the first guys there.

They carry me back to the bench, and as soon as the game was over, they took me over to emergency. And I went through x-rays and all that, and when the doctor came out, he says, "Well, I've got good news and bad news for you." I said, "Well, give me the good news first." He says, "The good news is you did not break any ribs today." I said, "What's the bad news?" He says, "When Jansen hit you three weeks ago, you broke two ribs." Oh yeah, I had the two broken ribs from three weeks before!

PART SEVEN

THE BAND AND MORE

One thing I learned very quickly after writing the *Tales for Michigan Stadium* books was that I had not included enough Michigan marching band stories. If I heard it once, I heard about it 100 times, so we corrected that problem in Part Two of that collection.

Another thing I learned while searching for Michigan band stories was that the band had the same kind of history and tradition as the football program. Additionally, those who participated in the marching band had the same love, respect, and emotional connection to the bands as football players had to the football program and coaches. As a player, I never fully understood the connection Michigan fans had to the band, either. It amazed me that some fans I spoke with came to the games mostly for the band, and the game was a bonus. The more I thought about it, I realized that Game Day is a lot more than just football—the band, the tailgates, and the total environment of the game day experience came under the umbrella of Michigan football. In this part of the *Voices of Michigan Stadium*, we explore that aspect of the Michigan football experience.

Starting with a band, you cannot begin a discussion without mentioning the father of the Michigan marching bands, William Revelli. Revelli served as the Director of Bands at Michigan from 1935 to 1971. In those 36 years, he became the Yost, Crisler, and Schembechler to the band program. Like those coaches, Revelli was a giant in his profession. He won international acclaim for insisting on musical precision. He was an innovator in synchronizing music and movement in large marching bands. He was the first to utilize a separate PA announcer to augment and make his band performance an understandable show for the fans.

Like those coaches, Revelli also became bigger than life—his demands to pay attention to detail and his insistence on discipline in his bands are legendary. And those standards are still in effect today as his lasting legacy. All you need to know about Bill Ravalli is revealed in this story from none other than Bo Schembechler himself, who got a visit early in his career from the great man.

Bo Schembechler*: All right, I came to Michigan nineteen-hundred and sixty-nine. I'm in my office, the first visitor that I get—absolute first visitor—William R Revelli. And he proceeds to tell me, he said, "I want you to know, I coach my band exactly the same way you coach your football team. We'll have discipline and we'll do it the way it's supposed to be done," and he goes on and on. And we talked for about a half an hour. I have never operated with a band of that caliber, you know, as coach. I mean, this is a precision machine, and it sounds great.*

So, when we came in early to practice, we brought him over and he'd come over and the band would play for us at the end of practice. You remember that? And then, I got to bringing him over when the freshmen came in early, and just the freshmen were here. And one night, we called to Bill Revelli, and Bill came over and he told the freshman—and, you know, he brought his pitch pipe, too—and he told them how this great fight song was written. And he said, "John Philip Sousa called this the greatest fight song ever." And he said, "You came into Michigan, and I can remember back when this guy played here, and that game over there." It was impressive. He knew football. He followed football. And then he would say, "All right, now, we're going to learn to sing The Victors!" And he'd make his note, and he'd tell them how to project your voice. He'd say, "You sing from down in here, and you'd let it out there you with feeling, and you do all this! Alright, let's go."

(Singing) Hail to the victors valiant! Hail to the conquering heroes! Hail!
Hail to Michigan…

And Revelli would interrupt, "Oh, no, no, no, that's not right. That's
terrible, there's no enthusiasm there! You don't sing it that way. When you
sing it, you got to mean it." And he'd go on and on. And I mean, it took
them a half hour to get through the song because every time they got to a
note he didn't like, Revelli would say, "No, no, no, that's the end of that.
We'll start over here. We're gonna get this right if I'm here all night!" He
was absolutely great. They loved it; those freshmen just loved it. And—and
every one of them came out of there—they knew the words, they knew how
to sing it, they knew how to emphasize, they knew how to do it—and it
was because Revelli came over there with the idea that those guys are going
to come out of here knowing how to sing this song, or else. And they did!
That's Bill Revelli."

Bo wasn't the first coach at Michigan that Revelli impressed. Going back
to the 1940s, Bill Revelli was making sure his band was getting their fair
shake at football games, sometimes to the irritation of head coach Fritz
Crisler. Long-time Michigan man Howard Wikel recalls when Revelli
and Crisler had conflicting agendas.

Howard Wikel: *I can remember many times when the team would*
come out of the locker room at halftime and Bill Revelli, his band was still
out on the field. Fritz would come out and say, "Come on, Bill, get them
off the field! We're gonna start the second half." And, you know, Bill timed
his thing right to the minute. He had a great, great band. I'm sure that he
was the father of the Michigan band. Fritz would have to kick him off the
field at halftime so we could start the second half. And now what irritates
me is, our bands are so wonderful that they leave with eight or ten minutes
left in the half."

Revelli was a special guy. Undoubtedly, he has a space on the Mount
Rushmore of Michigan bands. And it is amazing how his methods with

the band and the methods of his football counterparts were so very similar. Here's a story from one of the announcers Revelli hired to work the public address system. Carl Grapentine remembers an early incident with Revelli that illustrates the similarities.

> **Carl Grapentine**: *So, I auditioned for the legendary William Revelli; my first year was his last year. William Revelli was a genius. But like most geniuses, his mind just doesn't work like normal people, like you and me. And I remember one afternoon at a rehearsal, he was just reaming people out; he was on one of his famous tirades. And finally, he told them to just march up and down the field, just march up and down. It was like punishment for them. Everybody's being real quiet, because he's screaming, and I'm standing, like, six inches away from him while this is happening. It's my first experience with this; I don't really know what to do. So, I just sort of look at the ground and don't want to look up. So, they start marching up and down the field. Then, all of a sudden, I feel a tap on my shoulder. I think, "Oh God, maybe I'm supposed to go down and do that, too. I don't know. I'm new here." I look over and say, "Yessir?" And he's got his wallet out. He says, "Here's a picture of some fish I caught in Canada this summer."*

> *(Laughter)*

> *You wonder how much of it was an act sometimes, you know? But they're down there, sweating and getting yelled at, and he's showing me his fishing pictures."*

> *(Laughter)*

It was clear that Revelli put the band through its paces—he was tough! And what you see on the field in pregame, halftime, and postgame from this band is a reflection of the hard work Revelli put his band through to get it right.

One of the amazing facts about the band, that I never knew, was the extremely rigorous process they go through to get out there on the field and perform each Saturday. The process goes on to this day, and it was explained to me by former Michigan Drum Major Matt Pickus.

Matt Pickus: *There's 400 people in the band, you see 250 at halftime, and that's called the performance block, that 250. The rest of the group is called the reserves. But during band week, everybody looks at everybody else. The entire band votes on who makes the performance block and who doesn't. One rank at a time of 12 members marches in front of the marching band playing The Victors, and the entire marching band votes on who did better, who did worse, heads down, eyes closed. So, you're not really knowing what's going on. And that's how the performance block is set for the first game, is by a vote of the band. Instrumentation is taken into consideration by the staff, of course, and that's how it's set.*

But, three days into band week are the drum major trials. And the band votes by written ballot after a ten-event tryout—it's a decathlon, the candidates, one at a time, go up and there's an interview. You talk in front of the band about the two questions, and you're prompted beforehand, are, "What is the Michigan drum major?" and, "Why would you make a good drum major?" And then after that, one at a time, you go in front of the band. And candidate number one will show the position of attention, you stand up from the band, and then maybe you turn to the side, and then you turn around and you face the band, and you walk off. Candidate two, three, or whatever does that. So, there's the interview, position of attention, vocal commands, whistle commands, you then march—I think it's 15 or 20 yards of a low stride drill, you blow whistles, there's a percussionist behind you who takes up the tempo, and you march 20 yards. You then do the same thing with The Victors. You blow Victors' tempo, there's a percussionist, just one snare drummer behind you who will walk about 5 yards behind you as you march 40 yards. That's The Victors. It takes 40 yards to play The Victors.

After that, there's an optional twirling. You don't have to twirl, but pretty much everybody does. Then there is the entrance, which is the run onto the field, the turn to the left, the high kick in the back bend. And then, you know, the back-wind down to the plume. You're not wearing a hat, but you just go as far as you can. And then after the backbend, the entrance, the 10th event is "the strut." The high-kicking, leaning-way-back strut.

Then the band votes by written ballot, and you're elected then, and it's announced that night, and I tried out five years—I was in the marching band for seven years. And I am particular about one point, I got my undergraduate degree in four years and went immediately into grad school and stayed in the band. So, I lost my first tryout, and my second tryout, and my third tryout, and I came back and I won my fourth tryout. It was amazing, and it was phenomenal! And then the incumbents have to try out, too. And so, the incumbent has to come back and go through the whole thing. My second year, actually, nobody ran against me, I ran unopposed, but I still had to go through the 10 events."

Now, one of the traditional moments in pregame with the drum major is when he or she, during the M fanfare, struts toward the north endzone, removes the drum major hat, and does a deep backbend and actually touches their head to the ground. This feat of flexibility gets a huge roar from the gathered faithful, and it is impressive. But according to Pickus, this just doesn't happen overnight.

Matt Pickus*: And, you know, the tradition started in 1971 by Mark Brown. Legend has it, he's missing a couple of lumbar vertebrae, and he would bend over backwards, and that plume would touch between his heels. Nobody teaches you how to do these things—you work with past drum majors and you work with other marching band members. I worked with every single drum major from 1971 to me. I talked to Mark Brown, and I talked to Albert Arnheim—who used to do backflips instead of the backbend.*

I worked with every drum major before me, including going all the way back to 1950. I worked with Dick Smith; I called him up, the guy from the photograph, and I talked to him. I worked out with him on the field. And the first time I tried to do the back bend, the guy I was working with,

Ian Stein, kind of looked at me and he had these big, huge eyes, and he held his hands about half the height of the hat—maybe about 12 inches apart—and said, "You were that close to the ground." I though he was kidding! And after that it was, "Okay, can I get down and get up?" And then it was kind of, "Get down and get up, and make it look decent."

And my first tryout, I went out there and I touched my head to Elbell Field, and the whole band went nuts. I still lost, but when I did win, my first game was a week after I won, and I spent that entire week working with the band. And this is what's going on and—and the drum major's responsibility is, you get the band onto the field, such that they perform to the utmost of their potential. Everything else that you do is secondary.

So, I was concentrating on the band and everything was brand new to me. And we had rehearsals in the stadium, and it was 12-hour days during band week, and it comes time and I'm putting on the uniform and everything's fine. People are all excited, I'm tailgating with my mom and dad outside the stadium because they came up from Cleveland. And so, we marched to the stadium and it's wonderful. And we get into the tunnel, and everything is just great. And it's fun! And you're seeing the yellow and blue in the tunnel, and the teams go through, and you squish up against the wall. When the opponents come by you don't say a word and you look straight ahead, and it's dead silent in the tunnel. And then the Michigan team comes off the field and you're yipping around, and the percussion is playing and you're cheering, and then one of the marching band staff will look up and they'll say to the drum major, "Matt, bring him down!" and you run out of the front of the tunnel and you have the band members behind you. And you turn around and you're looking right at that snare drummer, and you're waiting for Carl's voice. Those four words that everybody loves, "Ladies and gentlemen, the Michigan Marching Band! Band, take the field!"

Then you start the cadence and you blow the whistle, and the band comes streaming out onto the field. And I'm doing all this and everything is fine. It sunk in that I was the drum major when I turned around and walked out to the sideline, because for the first 30-some odd seconds of the M fanfare, you've got nothing to do except stand there and look pretty. And all of a sudden, it sunk in, "What the hell have you done?" And, to this day, I will honestly tell you, I remember telling myself, "Don't run back into the tunnel. Don't." I was terrified! I was terrified.

I spent six years—five years—marching within the band, and I didn't march my first year; I was a reserve my entire first year, I never marched a game. And now I'm drum major! And I was terrified. And what's funny is, everything's fine. I went on my way, got out into the field, did the high kick, and we just decided that to get one game under my belt, I would leave the hat on because we weren't sure about how that would work and how often I would do it. So, that was the only backbend I did with the hat on. And I bent over backwards, and the hat's heavy, and I'm used to looking at the ground about three yards away from me, and with the brim of the hat, I'm now looking 30 yards away, and I lost my balance. So, I stood up, and I got set, and I went over backwards again, and I forget the plume. I smack the top of the head to the ground, and I get up, and I go on my way, and everything's great. And that was my first game.

The very next week, we played Notre Dame in 1993 at home, and some guy comes up to me, and he's poking his finger in my chest, and he's like, "So, how many times is it gonna take you to do the backbend today?" And he was real mad. And I was astonished. I looked at him, I said, "Sir, are you going to be in the stadium for pregame?" He said, "I haven't missed one in 30-some odd years." And he's just—and he's going off, and he's poking his finger in my chest. And I said, "You will see something today that has never ever been done before Michigan Stadium," and he's like, "Fine, I'll be watching," and he goes on his way, and I was still too nervous to pay attention to the crowd.

I went out there. Everything was fine before the game. I blew the whistle; the band is on the field. They're playing the M fanfare—it's the part in the M fanfare when the twirlers run off—I follow the twirlers, I take the corner, I do the high kick, and I take the hat off, and I put it on my hip. I bend over backwards; I touch all the way down to my head. I stand up, *flourish to the crowd, and I go on my way. I do the goalpost toss. I come off the field, and the guy who I worked with first, Ian Stein, he's on the trombone, he's on the other side of the field, he couldn't see me. And he comes up and he says, "What in the hell happened during pregame?" I said, "Why?" I had no idea what he's talking about. He said, "Because all of a sudden, the crowd got quieter than I've ever heard 'em, and then louder than it's ever been." I was too nervous to pay attention to the crowd. I came out and the crowd's going, "Hey, it's the drum major! He touches the plume to the ground! It's great! Wait, he's taking his hat off. What the hell is he doing? He's bending over backwards, no, he couldn't—" and it gets quieter and quieter, and I get about three inches from the ground. And I was watching the videotape after the game, and it's funny because Ian was absolutely right! There's this murmuring as I start bending over backwards, and it gets quieter and quieter. And I smack my head and they come up—and it got loud. That was my first hatless backbend.*

And two weeks later, there was a—there was a bye week or an away game. The next home game, I'm standing at attention in front of the stadium with a band behind me right outside the tunnel. And this guy walks up to me, and it's the same guy who scolded me after the opener. I was at standing at attention, and he says, "I know you're working right now. And you can't, like, say anything or move. But I'm sorry, man. That was just the most incredible thing I've ever seen!" And he walked away. I have no idea what the guy's name was.

Michigan band stories aren't exclusive to Ann Arbor, either. We heard earlier from band PA announcer Carl Grapentine about his first year with Bill Revelli. Well, let's spin ahead five years to 1976. Carl is now a seasoned veteran in the band public address game. So, he accompanies the band to Miami for the Orange Bowl. By the way, it's the first non-Rose Bowl game a Big Ten team participates in during the modern era, as the conference had finally eliminated their antiquated rule of limiting only one team from the conference to go to a bowl game. So, it was a big deal, and a huge game against Oklahoma. Carl got into the act early.

Carl Grapentine*: January 1ˢᵗ, '76, the Orange Bowl game, where I'm in the press box at the Orange Bowl before the Oklahoma game. It was some sort of an odd contraption where I had to wear a headset and hold on to a button or something, and so I was all hooked up and they were holding the game because—I think they were both on NBC back then—because the Rose Bowl was running late. That was the day that UCLA upset Ohio State out in Pasadena, knocking the Buckeyes out of number one. So, they were holding our start time. So, I'm sitting there and sitting there. Finally, we're seeing on a monitor that UCLA scored, whatever it was, to put it away. So, somebody came into the announcer booth and said, "We've got to announce the Rose Bowl score, because the people here don't know." And the guy says, "Well, you know, I got the Michigan band announcer all hooked up here and ready." And I said, "Well, I'll give it if you want!" And he said, "Okay." So, you know, I do this button and I say, "Fourth quarter score from Pasadena, UCLA-24, Ohio State-14," or something like that. And I'm expecting just a roar from this crowd, especially Oklahoma people. And there's not much reaction, so that's weird! But I'm in another one of those soundproof booths; maybe I just can't hear it.*

It wasn't until I got down to the field later on in the game, I'm walking over toward the band, they're saying, "Hey, Grape, way to go, way to go!" Turns out that when I did that Rose Bowl score, they were giving the invocation down on the field at the time—right in the middle of the prayer! And, you know, dear Lord, "Fourth quarter score from Pasadena…" I didn't even know that I had done it, of course, because of the soundproof booth. It was even—they even mentioned it in Sports Illustrated, they wrote, "Some overzealous PA announcer even thought to break into the prayer with the news."

While Grapentine's announcement was unavoidable because of the circumstance, there's a Michigan band story that left Ohio State with egg on their face, and they only have themselves to blame. The story comes from drum major Matt Pickus. On one particular Saturday in Columbus at Ohio Stadium, prior to the kickoff between Michigan and Ohio State, the Buckeye administration decided to have a pregame ceremony at one end of the field. When they told the Michigan band about this change, the band had to alter their positioning on the field for their pregame show. Because of this ceremony, the band didn't have the whole field to work with as was the norm—they only had 50 yards to work with. Well, it created an interesting situation for Pickus and where he would perform his deep backbend. Here's the way Matt explained it.

Matt Pickus: *The allotted time for the marching band was shorter than what we're used to. So, instead of coming out of the tunnel on the 50 and marching down to the endzone and playing The Victors, we came out centered on the 10-yard line and played the M fanfare. Instead of playing the beginning of The Victors, we went right to the trio and marched to the center of the field, and went on with the rest of our pregame. So, we shortened things a little bit. And my train of thought was—and I had warned the band before the game during announcements and everything else, I warned the band saying, "The crowd is going to boo, you've got to pay attention, you're not going to be able to hear anybody. They're going to announce the band, they're going to boo. They're going to announce the fanfare, they're going to boo. They're going to announce the Michigan man up front originally from Shaker Heights, Ohio, and they're going to boo! So, pay attention." And my train of thought was, "Well, if I'm coming out on the 10-yard line, where do I have to go? Because this is new, I've never figured this out before."*

I actually went through every single step where we started the 50 and I do the backbend on the 20. And that's 10 yards beyond where the flags are, which is—which is the furthest out group in the band. So, instead of turning right and going 30 yards, I'll turn left and go 30 yards, and that'll put me on the 40-yard line, so I know where I'm going. And then I thought to myself, "Well, the twirlers are on the left side of the field, and they only go five yards beyond the flags. So, if I'm gonna go 10 yards beyond the flag, I might as well go 10 yards beyond the twirlers, which puts me on the 45-yard line." And then I figured, "Well, hell, if I'm going to be that close…"

So, I went out, and I did the high kick and the hatless backbend and everything else, right in the dead center of the block O, absolutely. And that was my plan! So, they announce the Michigan band and the crowd boos, and they announce the fanfare and the crowd boos, and they announce, "From Shaker Heights, Ohio," and I'm standing in front of 235 people blowing their faces off, and I couldn't hear them! And I started to laugh!

On my resume to this date, in my little blurb about being twice-elected drum major of the Michigan marching band, it says, "frequently cheered by over 100,000 people, once personally booed by over 90,000."

So, I took the hat off and did the backbend, and it was dead silent except for the Michigan people cheering. Then I dropped into the splits and I flourished to the crowd, and they started booing again.

Michigan Stadium has such an amazing history, and it is historic as well. You just can't tell a complete story of the stadium without some non-football type tales. For instance, former PA announcer Howard King once had to prepare a speech about the stadium and its little-known facts. Whether truth or fiction, who knows, but King sure sounded convincing on this one.

Howard King*: In the mid 80s, I was asked by the Washtenaw Historical Society to do a presentation in the press box for the members of the society. So, I had two hours of material; they wanted it long and very comprehensive. You know, the stadium story is fascinating. Fielding Yost built this thing like a castle—maybe you didn't know that when this was poured with the concrete, that he personally inspected every load that came in. He had a chemistry professor inspecting the chemicals in the cement— in any case, he put six great big conduit openings from the press box down on the field site with absolutely no reason for them. He was smart enough to know that eventually there was going to be something that would need* *cable, so we don't have pulled cable. If you'll notice, a lot of schools have to pull it around or drape it, but ours is all right inside the stadium. It's a great thing!*

So, when I was doing this research—and this may be apocryphal—but I think it may also be true, but this stadium is built over Allen Creek, and there's a lot of quicksand in there. And they were bringing in fill... apparently, they brought in all kinds of fill, timbers and old cement. But the story is that as they were finishing up, a steam shovel was lost in the quicksand, and there's a steam shovel underneath Michigan Stadium right in the middle of the field, and it's in the stories. It's referred to in print that it's a true story. I don't know for sure, but it is quite possible, because I do know they brought load after load after load, trying to get this thing stable because it was a mess."

Did you also know that a private residence once existed inside the perimeter of the stadium? Yes, a private home was located on the southwest corner inside the fence of the stadium near the corner of Stadium and Main. Families lived there, too! One of the residents was equipment manager Henry Hatch. His daughter, Pat, was kind enough to tell me about growing up in the fishbowl of Michigan Stadium, and watching history being made right out your front window.

Pat Hatch*: One thing that stood out in my mind was standing at the south end of the stadium and watching President Johnson give the commencement speech. I think it was '64 that he did that. And then another thing that was kind of fun, was that we always locked the gate each night, you know, about 10 o'clock or so, and several times, as I remembered, there would be a knock at the door—after 10 o'clock—and there would be a couple that had come in and sat, you know, in the stadium there, and they were locked in and had to be let out. That was one of the interesting things. Game days were hectic. My mother, at the time, worked at the ticket office, too. And she was always at gate nine, and I remember there was a gentleman from Chicago that had made her acquaintance through the ticket* *office, and he would always bring his briefcase in and leave it at the house and then pick it up after the game. It was fun to sit there before the game and watch the crowds build and then just walk out my back door and walk over to my seat. I had a dear, sweet grandmother that just didn't see very well, but those were her boys down on the field. And because my mother was working, she and I would go over to our seats and she would sit there and cheer for Michigan.*

It would be a good feeling when it was empty on a moonlit night to walk out there and sit in a seat and just reminisce and think about things, just by myself. It would be in the evening usually, before I'd go to bed or something, and just sit there and enjoy the big scenery around, and the moon and all of that. So, it was pretty special.

Michigan Stadium was also the site of a cataclysmic change on the sidelines. Did you know that before 1974, Michigan did not have female cheerleaders? Only young men provided the cheering duties up until then, and they were mostly gymnasts. They would mark the score with backflips off the small brick wall that surrounded the field and perform various other cheers. But in the mid 1970's, athletic director Don Canham decided it was time to move forward and add women to the mix, like hundreds of other universities across the country.

Surprisingly, that decision didn't go over real well in Ann Arbor. It seems impossible today, but there was pushback at having female cheerleaders. The traditionalists were holding out, both from within the university community and from Ann Arbor. Canham chose one of his trusted staffers, Pat Perry, to implement the female cheerleaders program. And she told me it was a rocky start.

Pat Perry: *Then when it came time to get them to be cheerleaders, the boys kind of rebelled. And I was so frustrated that I had Newt Loken, who was in charge of the cheerleaders, and the fellows and meet with Don Canham, so we had both sides there. And Don said that this is going to come to pass and we are going to have girls on the field! And then the boys* *said, "Well, that's fine, but don't let them initiate a cheer! If we start a cheer, then they can join in at the other end of the field." And now, I look at how far they've come. It's really amazing!*

But the thing is, I had no budget, and I had to go scrounge for uniforms or something appropriate to dress the girls in so that they weren't necessarily always in—in their uniform. One time I borrowed waitress uniforms from Weber's restaurant. Another time I put an ad in the paper for those high-top white boots—go-go boots, I think they were called. Well, we had enough there for the girls, and I guess those boots were made for walking, however that song goes!

(Laughter)

Those are the few things that stand out in my mind. But I know I had to scrounge and borrow and beg and steal, practically, to get them in appropriate costumes."

One of the young women on that first squad of cheerleaders was Claire Canham, the daughter of Don Canham. She was just a college Co-Ed and looking to be part of the great tradition of Michigan. What she didn't see coming was the controversy the whole project would create. They even argued about what this group of young women would be called.

Clare Canham-Eaton: *It was not well received at the beginning, when it was announced. It was a huge break in tradition. So, a lot of the alumni weren't happy with it. The football men's cheerleaders weren't happy with it, and a lot of fans weren't happy with it. We were told that we were "pom-pom girls" and could not be called cheerleaders, and that we could not lead cheers. We could only join in on any of the cheers the men started and that we had pom-poms, and we were not to let go of our pom-poms for the entire game. That would make us pom-pom girls, not cheerleaders.*

And the funny fact about that is, they were metallic blue pom-poms. And after four hours, our faces and our hands and our legs all had been dyed blue. *Our uniform situation was unique. We had to start from scratch. Our basic game uniforms—we chose to look like the Southern California uniforms, who were the best cheerleaders in the country. They happened to be white, not maize and blue. They were white turtleneck-type uniforms with maize and blue stripes on them, and that was controversial because they should have been maize and blue in many people's opinions. The rest of the uniform situation was, we were halftime entertainment, and we had to wear costumes to work out with the band in George Cavender's halftime routine. And so, when Pat Perry talks about getting us costumes, they were truly costumes. We had Webber's waitress uniforms and go-go boots. At one point, we were dressed like Chiquita bananas.*

We also had to have our own our spot in the stadium, and that turned out to be good because the people around us were far enough away from the men cheerleaders, so they embraced us—except for that first game, when one of my cheerleading friends was hit in the head with a pop can. We had security the whole time, I think, because of the ongoing controversy about us. They were a little worried. And maybe the pop can incident was part of that. But we had two security guards go in and out of the game with us.

The only away game we went to was Columbus, and we stayed at a hotel the night before, which I think they turned off the water in the hotel for the team. If I remember, we were in the same hotel, and they were knocking on our doors all night as they were with the team. But we got dressed and we had a van, and we had a press parking pass where we were to park. So, we drive to Columbus, and we really don't know where we're going—it was before Google Maps—and we stopped a state police officer, and we showed him our parking pass, and we said, "Excuse us, officer, we don't know where we're going." And he put his head in the van and he saw 10 cheerleaders and white uniforms and he looked at the driver, which was a cheerleader, and he said, "The only place you can go to is hell."

So, our security guards actually took us out of the game early; we never saw the end of the game. They were concerned about us being on the field, so our security guards took us out. We got back in our van and drove home. But we stopped at a restaurant where we all went in, and we hadn't eaten all day, and we sat down and we waited, and we waited…and the waitress wouldn't serve us because we had on our Michigan cheerleading uniforms. People often ask what it was like, and we say, "At first we didn't really know that we were breaking tradition and making tradition all at the same time. We were all just honored to be a part of the university that we were all students at, and we loved. We felt very privileged, and it was a great honor to represent the University of Michigan."

Female cheerleaders are now, thankfully, just a normal part of the gameday experience. The other part of the gameday experience are the tailgates that occur all over Ann Arbor on football Saturdays. I can remember Leo Calhoun in his tailgate with murals of past Michigan football heroes painted on the side of his motorhome. He had mountains of food and he fed everybody that came by. Former players John Wangler and Dick Caldarazzo have joined forces for a super tailgate that welcomes anybody who wanders by, and has become a gathering place for former players of all eras.

But in the past, there were legendary tailgates that went above and beyond. One of those was put on by Ira Jaffe and Mel Lester. They had a corner outside the stadium tunnel, and they took tailgating to another level. Here's a sample of their monumental efforts in tailgating.

Ira Jaffe*: When we clean this up on Sunday morning, then I've got to make the inventory and get deliveries Wednesday and Thursday, take off all day Friday. Get up early in the morning to make the hot stuff. Get here, have a crew to set it up, and when we go home like two weeks ago, wash it 'til one in the morning so it's ready for the next day. There's 50 dozen donuts, I would say—20 to 30 pounds of corn beef, tuna, roast beef, turkey, salami, and I can keep on going. Everybody, you know, like, the messengers were here, some of the guards were here early. Friends, students who come up to us at weddings and say, "You don't know me, Mr. Jaffe or Dr. Lester, but you fed me for four years." It's really because we love life.*

Mel Lester*: I change the menu for every game; we never do the same thing twice. Today, there are 32 slabs of ribs, so there's about 400 ribs. I made 11 gallons of roasted tomato garlic soup. And my daughter, Stephanie, is the expert at chili. And we have about 15 gallons of chili here today. I do little tenderloin sandwiches, we do pastas, we do salads, depending on the weather, and it changes all the time. I think we probably feed up to between six-and-seven hundred for every game, now. Although, some people say it's gotta be 1000. I say, you know, when we got to 300, I lost count, and I don't bother. It's in your blood. I love it! It's a labor of love, and we would not miss it for a minute."*

As much as the volume of Mel and Ira's tailgate gets to me, there's one other tailgate I had to include because of what is served. It only happens for the last game every year, but the menu includes my favorite fish from my favorite Great Lake. Dave Schultz is the main chef. It started small but, man, has his tailgate exploded over the years.

Dave Schultz*: Well, 25 years ago, when I got invited to this—I come from Northern Michigan, and they had all this great food and beverage, and I wanted to bring something that was unique from where I grew up. So, I brought a dozen filets of perch with a single burner Coleman stove. And now, today, it's 2000 filets the last game every year, and my dad migrated from the city and built a small marina on Saginaw Bay on a dead-end road. Now, our family owns all the commercial fishing licenses in Saginaw Bay and Lake Huron. So, we share the wealth.*

I was born blue! And, yeah, there's a special recipe, and I'll tell it to you. It's 60% Kellogg cornflake crumbs, 40% flour, the spices that you and your friends like. But the key is, the grease is 350 to 375 degrees, whether there's wind or no wind. Take the wind at your back, then two to three minutes, depending on the size of the fish, is how you cook it. We love it! Everybody loves it! When I come the first game every year, people ask, "You're gonna bring the perch for the last game, right?" Who cooks 14 dollar-a-pound perch in the parking lot in Ann Arbor? We do!

PART EIGHT

BO, IN HIS OWN WORDS

We've been blessed at Michigan to have so many legendary personalities lead the football program. Each and every one of them were unique and exceptionally talented in their own way. They were also all very quotable! But, because of the time that he presided as head coach, Bo Schembechler has a special place in the array of talent in the Michigan football tradition.

His unique popularity may have also been a product of those times; the electronic media was beginning to emerge, and Bo's personality played perfectly into the growing electronic environment of sports coverage. He was opinionated, he was gruff, he was confrontational. He could be playful and very funny. He was, very simply, good copy, and a great soundbite just waiting to happen. In the end, Bo Schembechler was special. When he spoke, you couldn't help but listen. He commanded your attention, whether telling a joke or admonishing you for a mistake. I've never met anyone like him, and I haven't met anyone since that's close. That's why this section is simply called, *Bo, In His Own Words*. There's just something compelling about his ability to tell a story or relate an event. So, sit back and enjoy Bo at his best.

This first example comes courtesy of Cam Cameron, and assistant coach to Bo. After Bo had died, I was helping his widow, Cathy, clean out Bo's office at Schembechler Hall, and we came across some audio cassettes that were just labeled, "Bo Pregame." Cathy said to me, "Why don't you take them?" and I said, "Fine." They spent the next two years in my garage in a file box called *Bo*.

When I started this project, I pulled these tapes out and learned they were recorded by Cameron during Bo's last year as coach. For some reason, Cam wanted a record of a pregame talk from Bo to his team. Well, *thank you, Cam!* Because now we all have the good fortune of hearing Bo from the locker room at Illinois in 1989 address his troops before they took the field against the Illini.

Bo Schembechler*: Now, you cover because, you know, we've been working hard on the protection. And you've got to understand, you got a return guy back here that's good and, they could be holding us up—make sure you read rush or return! Cover is important, because the same thing could very well happen to them, where they're concerned with their punt protection. We could be ripping a punt back on them just as easily as not. We want to make sure that on other kicking situations, such as the kickoff return, and the kickoff coverage, that you block and cover the return. Let's get a big play out of the returns, let's get one, let's get one—we got one last week, let's get one this week. Maybe this week, it's a punt return. But let's get those kickoff returns because, I can't overemphasize the importance of field position after you receive a kickoff. That is important. So, block your ass off and get after it!*

And let's block a kick—I'd like to see a punt blocked, an extra point blocked, field goal blocked; let's block a kick! Let's go after one and get it. We've worked hard on it, we ought to be able to do that. All right, that's basically what we have to do in the kicking game, because we must win the kicking game. We must win the kicking game; this is going to be vitally important to the success of this game. We've got to play our ass off and accept that responsibility.

And we are a better special teams' team than they are! Let's go after this team and get it done. You all understand, defensive players and everybody, that we cannot, and will not, and must not accept the tie in this game.

We take nothing but victory! There is our two-point play already set to go for it. If we have to go for it, we will. I want you to know that if the circumstances are such, that if we tie, they're going to go to the Rose Bowl—you know that as well as I do. We cannot tie. We must win this game. And that's what we're at. Any questions about that?

All right, now…we are overdue to play a big game. That's what this is all about. It's exciting! And everybody, I'm sure—coaches, players, everybody—are ready to play another big one. And this is the big one! I want you to know, when you go out there, you've got that nervous energy, you're ready to go, you're anxious to go, you use that nervous energy! But you do it while you're thinking.

You're a thinking ball club. You go out there with confidence that you can beat this team anywhere you play them, anytime, anyplace—that's the way we feel about any team that we oppose in the Big 10 conference. We'll beat 'em anytime, anyplace, anywhere. But we got to play our best, and in order to play our best, we just have to think our best. We got to be smart. We got to know what we're doing. We got to be aggressive as hell on defense. We got to throw downfield, we got to sustain the blocks. We got to run and get the last yard, the absolute maximum last yard we can get.

We got to do everything that a champion does. Because, keep in mind, gentlemen, when you take the field at Illinois, you are the champions of the Big 10 conference. You are the cream of the Big 10 conference. And nobody can take that away from you if you don't want it, 'cause you're good enough to do it again. And we had as our goal to repeat, to repeat, and now we have to stand up and be counted. And we're gonna do it right out here in Illinois. Now, let's go!

We'll close this section of Voices with another pregame talk from Bo little later. But for now, let's hear from Bo and some of his more interesting comments on his career at Michigan. In his first year, one of the most difficult losses he ever experienced came in East Lansing against Michigan State. He admits it was not pretty.

Bo Schembechler*: It was bad coaching that lost the game, there's no question about it. We were just fooled. And I'll never forget this until the day I die. Jim Young was our defensive coordinator—great coach—and, of course, Jim was frustrated because they had jumped from the wishbone to the I formation. We had all wishbone defenses, and they jumped to the I formation, and they were marching up and down the field. And I walked up the sideline, I grabbed him by the arm, and I said, "Jim, for God's sake, let's get them stopped!" And he turned around, looked at me, and his face turned white, and he fainted right there in front of me. He fainted! We had to revive him and get him up. I'm sure you recall that—you were probably on that team up there and saw that. But anyway, that was my indoctrination to the Michigan State series."*

In one season, Bo took some flak for beating Illinois 70 to 21. Some in the media suggest that he was running up the score; Bo never let the critics faze him, though.

Bo Schembechler*: Anybody that got beat by 70 points is gonna say you run it up, heaven's sake. 70 points! Truth of the matter is, we were scoring with the third guys and the fourth guys; we were scoring with everybody late in that game.*

Another classic Bo moment came after an Illinois game in 1985. Michigan went into Champaign and came away with a disappointing 3-3 tie. Schembechler, at his motivational best, knew exactly the path to take in his postgame talk to his team.

Bo Schembechler*: When we tied that game and came into the locker room, and our players were so distraught, I called them all together. And I said—and I was emotional—I said, "Hey, we went into this snake pit, but they couldn't beat us. And we may not have played as well as we can play, but we played hard. We have nothing, absolutely nothing to be ashamed of. And I'm going to tell you one other thing; there's nobody going* *to beat us the rest of the year. Nobody! I don't care what bowl we go to or what we do, no one will beat us the rest of the year."*

And I think if you go back through the record, nobody beat us. Because that team at that time proved that it was a close-knit group. I mean, they were—they were a tight knit group. And when they saw that I had faith in them, after being tied—embarrassingly tied—in Champaign, Illinois, they really did a job. So that was a good football team! That was a good one."

Bo's postgame, pregame, and halftime speeches have always been portrayed a little different than Bo himself thought of them. As a matter of fact, he found the characterization of his fire and brimstone halftime talk somewhat humorous.

Bo Schembechler*: The halftime speech is a misnomer, because it doesn't happen at halftime. You don't have time for that at halftime. At halftime, you have to make adjustments, and you're busy with the technical aspect of football. If you want to motivate, to stimulate, it may come during the week. It may have come before you left the hotel, to come to the locker room to dress. Those speeches, they come from time to time when you think they're necessary, that's when they come. But halftime speeches, per se— unless you're really mad about something, which has happened on occasion, and the results very often have been positive—but there's no such thing as the old pregame, halftime, "Let's go win one for the Gipper!" speech. No, I don't see those much, anymore.*

While Bo had offensive coordinators during his career, make no mistake, Bo had a great deal to say in the offense every year he coached. He was an offensive coach. He loved defense, don't get me wrong, but he felt he could control the game with his offense, and that's where he wanted to be. In order to control an offense, the head coach and the quarterback had to have a special relationship. Through all the ups and downs, the coach and quarterback had to be in sync, and Bo made it clear to any player who played quarterback for him, that there was just one simple rule.

> **Bo Schembechler**: *They boo every quarterback, they boo coaches, you know, there's always a little booing. There's not a lot in Michigan Stadium, but there's always a little. I always told the quarterbacks this so that—so that they understood that this may happen. There is only one guy in the entire stadium that they have to please, just one. Now, if I don't like what they do, they're in trouble. If 105,000 hate his guts, and boo him, it doesn't mean damn. And he's got to understand that. So, I tried to indoctrinate these quarterbacks so they know that, just take care of Ol' Bo, and you're all right.*

One of those quarterbacks Bo had a great relationship with was Jim Harbaugh, the current Michigan coach. On one occasion—you probably all remember—against Ohio State, Harbaugh hooked up with John Kolesar on a huge pass play when the game was still in doubt for a touchdown to stop an Ohio State rally. Bo saw that play coming all the way.

> **Bo Schembechler**: *We anticipated the blitz because once they got back in the game, they had decided that they were going to come after us every down, particularly second and long. So, they came with the strong safety. The strong safety came, and we did not get a helmet on him; he was not blocked. And this little Jimmy Harbaugh stood back in there, Kolesar ran right past their best defender. And Jimmy looked at that strong safety, who's going to hit him right under the chin and knock him flat, and pinpointed that ball into Kolesar for a big play and a touchdown. And that took the wind out of their sails!*

It always seems to be Ohio State that brings out the best or the worst, doesn't it? In Bo's case, maybe the most controversial and disappointing moment of his career came following an Ohio State game. The year was 1973, Michigan and Ohio State had played to a 10-10 tie in Ann Arbor.

The tie had also tied them for the Big 10 title. Michigan had outplayed Ohio State decidedly in the second half of the game, outgaining the Buckeyes 209 yards to just 91. Despite the tie score, the consensus of those watching had the Wolverines as the better team. Even Buckeye coach Woody Hayes admitted that Michigan should go to the Rose Bowl as the Big 10 Representative.

But late in the game, Michigan's talented quarterback Dennis Franklin had broken his collarbone. The aftermath of the injury was that some felt he would not be ready to play six weeks later in the Rose Bowl. The Big 10 athletic directors had a telephone conference call the night after the game to vote on who they felt should get the nod and go to the Rose Bowl to represent the conference. It was a foregone conclusion that Michigan would get the nod; they had outplayed Ohio State. Additionally, the Buckeyes had played in the Rose Bowl the previous year. It was Michigan's year.

Shockingly, the athletic directors voted to send Ohio State. There was outrage from the Michigan faithful. The injury to Franklin was the rumored reason why the AD's voted for Ohio State. It was senseless, not to mention, completely unfair. Dennis Franklin recalls the situation.

Dennis Franklin: *Walking off the field, we went right into the locker room, you know, Dr. O'Connor started playing around with my collarbone and at one point, he started mashing down on it. And it slipped—I mean, went back into place. And I tell you, Jim, I never felt pain like that; at that moment, I felt like I was dead. I mean, I wanted to scream, like, I just couldn't really believe it, and you could actually hear the bone go back together. It was just horrible! But he did it—set it right in place.*

From that point on, it didn't really hurt. And so, you know, I had to go through the four-to-six weeks, whatever it takes to heal. I just remember that at that moment, I felt like it's not going to be that difficult to play in the Rose Bowl. I didn't even think that we wouldn't be going to the Rose Bowl. I mean, it was a 10-10 tie, we had a chance to win, we clearly were the better team. The last thing I thought about was us not going to the game. So, you know, I went through it, took some time off. I went home for Thanksgiving, but they really didn't give me an opportunity to demonstrate that I would be well by the time it was Rose Bowl time. It's crazy, very disappointing.

And, you know, to this day, you know, the thing that hurts the most is, like, now there's so many memories of that particular game and the 10-10 tie. And we should have had an opportunity. This is my first experience at the Rose Bowl thing. Being out here and seeing the guys and players go out to practice, I never experienced that. And none of the guys that were my year, not only here—which is the granddaddy of them all—but any other bowl game for that matter. So, it's just, like, seems like it's so unfair.

For Schembechler, the vote in '73 was the lowest point in his career. Til' he died, he never forgave, and he never forgot.

Bo Schembechler*: There were some very weak character guys in athletic director positions in the Big 10; that's been proven. And everybody thought, "Well, you know, we'll let it go and forget about it." But I had some great football players with great teams that never got to play in that great classic. They were some of the best football teams in the United States of America. And I never forgot that—I never forgot that. I always said to myself, "If I ever let up on my bitterness over what happened to that football team in 1973, I'm not being fair to those guys who played." And so, I never have. And I've been bitter ever since about it. And, and I'll never—I'll never forget it, as long as I live.*

And fortunately, as a result of that situation, we took the determination of the Rose Bowl representative out of the hands of the athletic directors, because they weren't qualified to handle it. And second of all, because of that Michigan team in 1973, all these other teams in the Big 10 conference now have an opportunity to play in a postseason bowl game, because that restriction of the Rose-Bowl-or-no-bowl was as antiquated and stupid as anything the Big 10's ever done. And so, we did accomplish something— but it was at a hell of an expense.

This is a perfect spot for another pregame speech from Bo during the '89 season. This game against Purdue was played 16 years after the infamous 10-10 tie vote. But you can tell in Bo's message that taking anything for granted is a major mistake. His intensity was palpable. Bo wanted his team to know that leaving the decision up to somebody else is dangerous; take the decision into your own hands by your actions and your play.

Bo Schembechler: *When you go into a game like this—we talked about this—it's all about our approach and our attitude and how important that is, in a confrontation like this. I wrote down here that this will be a physical confrontation; I promise you, it will be. They'll be very physical. They'll come after you, and they'll be a physical game. I like that because that will bring out the best in us. But we must be thinking properly at all times. We are going to go out and play as hard as we can, we're going to start fast, we're going to say that this game is just as important to us of all the games we play in terms of winning the championship. Because if we don't beat Purdue, there is no championship. There is nothing for us, nothing.*

So, we don't take anybody lightly, because we have to win them all. When we go out there offensively, defensively, kicking, going under kicks—everything; start fast! Start fast! Never give the sucker a break. Never give them the thought that, "Maybe Michigan don't want to play today. Maybe they don't want to play today, and we got a shot." Don't ever give them that. You go down there, everybody going all out in this game. And then, by God, they'll understand that we're going to win the championship! And we're going to the Rose Bowl, and nobody else in this league is, and we are the dominant team in this league.

And we do it every week. Consistency is important to us every single week. And what we did last week doesn't mean anything, unless we do the same thing over again, only better. We must improve. Alright, let's go!

These pregame talks are so great because Bo was so good at it. He was emotional, and yet business like. He balanced the X's and O's perfectly with the enthusiasm he needed to impart to play in a physical game. I was always amazed that he used notes, but never a script. He spoke off the top of his head, and yet had great focus and organization in his messages. He could scare you, he could make you laugh, he could make you mad—and he could pull you and push you through just about every emotion, and you always came back for more. I asked him once, "How much of it was an act?" And while his answer surprised me, it made perfect sense.

Bo Schembechler: *Sure, I can act. Sure, I can act! I'm very disappointed that no one from Hollywood has seen fit to contact me, but—*

(Laughter)

—The truth is, that if you have a cause, and you want to express yourself because of something that happened and you want to make sure that you're heard, you're going to act and get it done. I think any coach who can't act, can't coach—because what does he do before a team? What do you do before team? Aren't you presenting some material to them in a way in which it's going to excite them and make them listen, and make them want to learn? Of course, you are! And when you do that, aren't you going to be animated? Of course, you act! Anybody who's ever been before the public acts. Anybody who's trying to make a point is an actor. So, if that's the case, then I'm an actor!

Of all the decisions he made at Michigan, the toughest one for Bo came in 1989. It was no act, either. For a number of reasons, after twenty-one seasons as Michigan's coach, Bo decided to retire.

Bo Schembechler: *I'm sad at leaving; I hate to leave the players, I hate to leave coaching. But it's time to go. The doctor, particularly Dr. Reicher, had been pushing me to slow down. That, you know, "You just can't keep going, you're going to be 60 years old. You can't just keep pushing yourself like this." And as he related, he said, "I don't think that you'll ever be able to step back and take a lesser role, because you're too conscientious. You're just not the kind of person that can do that. The only* *way you're going to be able to do this thing is to divorce yourself from the athletic program."*

It just dictated to me that it was time to go. And when I made the decision to retire, I never looked back. It was the right thing to do. It was the right time to do it. What other football coach that coached a major college team could walk away from the job that he loved the most? I'll never have a job like the one I left. It was the most gratifying that I'll ever have. But to be able to walk away with the idea that I kept it intact as I left—it was not in disarray; I was not chased out of town. There were not violations of recruiting rules that forced me to resign. And all of the great people that contributed to the twenty-one years that were still with me, are still working here doing the same thing they did under me. That is unheard of in intercollegiate athletics, and to be able to do that made me very, very proud!

But I'll never have a job like that again. I'll never—you just don't come on these jobs. I mean, it could have been somebody else that got the Michigan job in 1969 and probably done the same things that I've done, maybe even better. But they wouldn't have the respect for the job like I had. I mean, I just—it was the best thing that ever happened to me in my life.

PART NINE

THE MICHIGAN EXPERIENCE

The most amazing component of Michigan Stadium is the emotional aspect of the place that each and every player or coach feels as they remember their days in this great arena. As I was putting this project together, one of the questions I asked everyone was to recall a feeling that you've never had before or since, that you experienced with Michigan football. Without hesitation, almost everyone had a story or a sense of being a part of history when they thought back to their days as a Wolverine. It didn't matter what year or what era the player came from; the same sense of awe and inspiration was realized by them all. I call it "The Michigan Experience."

Terry Barr played at Michigan back in the mid 1950s. One of Michigan's all-time greats, Barr was asked years after he graduated to address the football team. To prepare for this talk, Terry told me he reached out to other players to get a sense of their experience, and it confirmed for him something he already knew.

Terry Barr: *I was speaking to the team and so, I wanted to get a feeling of what I know—what we felt. I just picked out a whole bunch of guys and called them on the telephone, that played for Michigan going back several years. And it was fun! Some of them talking on the phone, some of them wrote me letters, but it was unbelievable. Guys, you know,* *like—a doctor here, and this guy's that, you know what I mean? And they all took time. I think there're, like, only three guys that didn't write me, and I treasured that to this day. I got some of those things, and I thought to myself…I was not amazed by it. Rather, it confirmed for me more than amazing me, that this isn't a new feeling for guys that played football at Michigan—not at all! No matter what their years said on their jersey, no matter what, they all have the same feeling and love for the university; it's a unique place in that regard. It was one thing to go to practice and then you go out and…but it's a whole different ballgame when it's game time. You go out on the field, I mean, I—when I think back on it, I mean, I hardly remember my feet touching the ground.*

To this day, I am so proud when people ask me, "Well, where did you go to school?" I mean, I can't wait to get it out of my mouth, "Michigan!" And that's been that way with me since forever. And I'm sure it will stay that way. You know, there's an unbelievably special place to take me forever to really say how I feel about Michigan and what it's meant to my life. I met my wife there. My friends that I spend most of my time with now are guys that went to college years, years ago.

Fast forward to the late 1990s. Over half a century later, Tai Streets, another Michigan great, has a similar story—only, Tai's love affair began even before he enrolled at Michigan.

Tai Streets: *I didn't know, cause I was watching on TV. You don't get the feeling until you actually go there. And I went and sat in the crowd in my junior year of high school, it was just amazing. And then when I first walked in when it was empty, we went there I think at night like a couple of nights before our first game, the Virginia game in 95 and it was amazing. You just get that feeling when you walk in and man it is just an incredible feeling. I don't know how to describe it. That was a great experience in my life, including the professional ranks getting paid and all that. Man, there's nothing like four years in Michigan. Just the memories* *of touching that banner. Coming down hearing that crowd roar. It's just the greatest feeling. If anybody has a choice to go to college, I don't know why they wouldn't make Michigan one of their choices, just the greatest place you could ever play.*

Back in the 1940s, Bob Chappius had an emotional moment in the stadium he'll never forget—and remember, this is coming from a guy who was the leader of the famous Mad Magicians of Fritz Crisler's National Championship team—whose life experience included having the plane he piloted being shot down during World War II, who spent time surviving behind enemy lines. So, when you read this, you'll get an idea of just how special the Michigan Experience is.

Bob Chappius*: Oh, I'll tell you, I never will forget that after the Ohio State game, walking up that tunnel. I couldn't believe it! It was like, this can't be the last time I'm gonna play here, it just can't be! But it was, and at least we had the Rose Bowl to look forward to. But nonetheless, that stadium…*

I remember we were playing Army in 1946. Blanchard and Davis, and of course, they beat us 20 to 13. But I remember coming out at halftime, and the band was still on the field and they were playing the alma mater and I stood there next to Bruce Hilkene and I had tears running down my cheeks. And I thought, gee whiz, I can't do this, and I looked at Bruce, and there were tears running down his cheeks too. And that was so, you know, I'm an emotional guy anyway, I never will forget that. And of course, the first time running down against that Great Lakes team was really special to me, to look up and I see all those people, I thought, my gosh, isn't this something. You know, you just can't believe it. You can't believe the grip that that stadium has on you."

Sometimes, the Michigan Experience makes itself known in the oddest of ways. For Michigan's great defensive tackle Bill Yearby, it came to him on a beautiful Saturday afternoon.

Bill Yearby: *I'll tell you a great story. I was a sophomore we played against Navy, we played Roger Staubach and he was a great quarterback. And he was a scrambler. I was a young person. And I had a lot of energy that day. And you know, I was always on it. Right before halftime, they ran an off-tackle play. I didn't remember anything afterwards. I looked up. It was a hot, sunny day. And I could remember saying what a beautiful looking sky! I remember thinking, wow! Then the trainer was saying, "What's your name?" I was thinking, "Who are you?" I didn't know anything after that. I was knocked out. But when I came to, I was looking at the sky and it was the most beautiful thing I've ever seen. And I will never forget that because I realized what had happened. I was saying, "Man, if I was unconscious, maybe I could see a whole lot of beautiful sky!"*

That was a great thing, you know, it was—it was a tremendous time that, during that time, because I think we were about building a program up here, and we were successful at it. It was just something as I watched the teams now, it's just amazing because, you know, I always feel a part of it. And it's always exciting!

I never will forget Ron Kramer and Jim Pace. All of those guys that played up here because as a kid I used to watch them, you know, and I never thought that I would get that opportunity to play at Michigan, but I was just so surprised and grateful that I did.

It's funny how the weather had an impact on Yearby and his Michigan experience, because Gordon Bell, one of the Wolverines' finest running backs, had a similar moment that sealed the deal for him.

Gordon Bell: *It was funny, it was the Ohio State-Michigan game. It was my senior year we came up for a recruiting trip. We drove up here and there was like four kinds of weather. It snowed, it rained, it sleeted, and then hailed, and then right before the Michigan team came out, they were sweeping the field because the field was white, completely white.*

So, they squeegeed the field and you can see the field was green. I was at the top of the stadium and I looked out over the over the campus. I said you know what, I really liked this place it's like I fit in. And just when the Michigan team was coming out of the tunnel, the sun started to shine and hit the gold pants, the blue jerseys and I was like, this is it! Sunshine. It was like it was like I knew I was supposed to be here.

For others, The Michigan Experience wasn't about the weather. It was about how a physical change came over you. Tight end Craig Dunaway talked about the moments before a game that still puzzle him.

Craig Dunaway: *When you come out of that tunnel, and there's this sea of people. It's just, it's unbelievable. I mean, you realize, holy smokes, all these folks are here to see what you know, I'm part of and, and it's just it really it gives you goosebumps. I mean, I remember before almost every game as the crowds filling in and you know that last bit of warmups you do before you go in the tunnel and then come out the final time. I would remember getting ready for you know, just doing your things running through your drills, whatever, just kind of breaking a sweat. And it was I could feel like I was almost hyperventilating. You know, just the adrenaline's pumping, you got a little bit of that nausea that you get with that. And you sweat—I don't know, I just I sweat, you know, sweating profusely and think, "Oh my God, am I out of that out of shape? I'm short of breath!" It's got to be just—it is, you know, it's the butterflies and the, you know, the hum of the crowd is the, you know…as you get closer and closer to the game. And it's, you know, it didn't never happen on the road. It happened just in Michigan Stadium. I mean, it didn't happen when I went to Pittsburgh and played in Three Rivers or wherever, you know, we'd go there. I mean, it was it was something about Michigan Stadium that you got ready for a game in a different way.*

For Dunaway, it was a physical thing. For another great Wolverine, Braylon Edwards, it was a mental thing. Braylon told me for his first game at Michigan, he was a basket case—the adrenaline had completely taken over!

> **Braylon Edwards**: *I was jacked up out of my mind. I just had never been in a situation like that, feeling so much anxiety and so much was ready to burst out in me, and I was, like, I was glad I wasn't starting because I probably would have jumped offsides. I was so nervous, but I finally actually got a chance to get a catch in that game.*
>
> *My first game ever, I had two catches. It's just great. It's like you're walking on air. You know, when I touched the banner, I thought I was gonna jump over the banner. It's just a lot of fun. All I could tell myself was don't knock the banner down. Don't knock the banner down. It's just a great feeling to be a part of that. Running out there and seeing all these fans, 107,000 strong, so it's just great that I had a chance to be a part of it.*

Believe it or not, Braylon's father Stan, another Michigan standout, had a similar experience to his son. When I asked Stan about his memories of Michigan Stadium, without knowing what son Braylon had told me, Stan said this.

> **Stan Edwards**: *When I think of Michigan Stadium, and me playing in Michigan Stadium, it always goes back to the very first time. My freshman year, the very first home game, we came and ran out the tunnel, and I sat in the stands probably two years prior being recruited up there. But it was so different.*
>
> *We played our first home game my freshman year, we started down the tunnel. I mean, this is even after we went out for pregame warmup, when we started down the tunnel and you know the stadium is full, and at the top of the tunnel you can hear the guy on the PA system, he's introducing the other starting lineup, and the tunnel seems so—the opening seems so small, and you just start down like a herd of cattle. And then it's kind of like, "Oh my God, I've been working for this this all my life, and it's here!"*

And when we finally went out, and I'm at the back, because I'm a freshman, and we go out to go up and touch the banner, I took probably two steps on the field and completely stopped. I could not hear anything. I just stopped and start staring in the stands. I was thinking, "Oh my God!" And it was quick thinking by somebody who grabbed me and said, "C'mon, let's go, let's go!" And I kind of shook out of it.

When I jumped up to the banner and went off to the side and jumped into the pile, and then after we broke the huddle again, I just stared. And I was probably looking around the stadium, and after probably about the first two series, I wasn't playing. And the first couple of series I just spent just looking in the stands. I'm like, "This is amazing!" And it's probably good I didn't play, because I probably wouldn't have made a play. And I was so amazed that this is actually it. So that was kind of my first case of how big it could be. Oh my God, I literally froze!

The run out from the tunnel and under the banner for the first time is clearly a special Michigan experience. For some, like nose guard Tim Davis, it was unreal.

Tim Davis: *I think more or less, I was like in a dream more than anything else. When I ran out there, and I just saw the wave of people, I could not believe that this many people were watching me or the football team that I played for, which was Michigan, and it was just overwhelming. It was it was like a dream. I'll be honest with you, that's how it felt to me, and I was glad I was with Michigan.*

It wasn't just Tim Davis who had the dream state happen to him. The great Rick Leach explained what his memories were about during that special experience.

Rick Leach: *To get the equipment on, to get the helmet with the home jerseys, and I'll never forget, I always tell people I don't think I felt my feet until, you know, probably sometime in the middle of the first quarter* *to come on the field with that kind of crowd with the band's playing, the enthusiasm and excitement. I mean, I'll never forget that. You couldn't replace that kind of adrenaline and motivation anywhere. I mean, I don't care what you do, you can just never replace that!*

Trying to convey how special Michigan is can be a trip through many different aspects of a player's experience. One of the best explanations of how different it is, came from former Wolverine John Kolesar

John Kolesar: *First of all, it's just overwhelming. I mean there's just no words. People are always asking, and you tell them the best story you can, but you can never ever really tell them how you really felt.*

There are aspects to the stadium, there's a few things in the locker room before the game, and I'm not sure if you remember—I think it's changed now because of the new locker room—but you remember the tunnel between the locker room and Crisler, I used to sit in that tunnel by myself before a game and just focus on getting into the zone. And I just drew on the ghosts, I guess, from Yost. And, you know, when I put that helmet on and I hit the Go Blue Go sign, it's almost like you had a force. It's almost like you were invincible.

To go through your mind and your body physically were just kind of together. And it was—just worked. It was like the final piece of the puzzle of the week of practice and going through there. And I liked it, because when I went to the pros with the Buffalo Bills, it was entirely different experience.

Okay, I mean, we can talk about that for hours. But one of the big things I was relying on was Game Day—and we had a game against Denver Broncos, Monday night game. We're talking the epitome of NFL football. All right, I'm ready to go. I'm excited. Monday Night Football. We're gonna get out there we're gonna play and I go do my pregame ritual. You know, put your socks on the right way and things. And I go—I once I put my strap on and I buttoned up and I tightened down my helmet. And I get in the tunnel, and right when you get to the opening of the tunnel is when you know the magic kind of explodes. Well, in Buffalo, it didn't. So, I go out, and I was excited because I was kind of struggling through training camp and this is a whole different world than Michigan football and I get out there. I see 80,000 screaming Buffalo fans looking down, and I'm like--oh my God, I'm waiting, and I'm waiting, and nothing! That's what it was. And it was just disappointing. The aspects of the game which I love, and I tried to develop, did not measure up to Michigan Stadium.

There's so much emotion that is expended during a game, and that emotion is doubled by the prospect of being at Michigan Stadium. You're wearing that uniform; you're wearing that helmet. For one of Michigan's all-time best running backs Butch Woolfolk, that moment was frightening.

Butch Woolfolk: *It was really, really scary. I remember early on in the season, sitting on the bench, I really wasn't part of the game because freshman knew they weren't going to play. But then when I got on the field, it was so scary. We were sitting in the I formation, I'm back there dotting the I, and the fullback is in front of me and Rick Leach is in front of him. I couldn't hear anything. And if he changed the play, I'd be lost. And I would just sit there and move when everybody else moved because I couldn't hear anything. I tell you that game. The first game that I played was the most exciting game I've ever had in Michigan Stadium. I was green I didn't know what I was doing. I just follow Rick Leach's lead and Russell Davis's lead. They told me what to do on every play. They calmed me down in the huddle and I was really scared about that game. I was kind of numb. I was numb about the whole thing. The fear was messing up in front of Michigan Stadium and the fear was also coming in as a freshman trying to please Bo and appease Bo because he didn't want to play me. I know he didn't want to play me. I figured if I made a mistake, it would just be worse.*

Another first game that was a little different than Woolfolk's happened for linebacker Tom Stincic, back in 1966. In his first start, Stincic told me it was an eye opener, not for the speed of the game or the fans in the stands or the quality of play—Tom said it was about his teammates and the example they set for him that lasted a lifetime.

Tom Stincic: *First game I started as a sophomore, Oregon State. They had a huge receiver with basketball player size, six-foot-eight. I was fortunate to play with some defensive backs that were seniors, John Rowser, Rick Volk, Mike Bass, Dick Sygar. And they had in their mind that this guy wasn't going to catch a pass. And I was just real wide eyed, first game, big time, all that stuff. I was 18 years old. They made this guy's life miserable. They tattooed him, they hit him. And, in our huddle, I can still remember them saying, "It's your turn, you go over and you just hit him. So, when I hit him, then you come and hit him." And I was thinking, "Oh my gosh, there's going to be a fight, we're gonna get penalties!"*

I was just in awe, because here was this guy, and when I stood next to him, he was six-foot-eight, 230 pounds or whatever he was—and that was my first memory of, you know, "Hey, I'm playing with some real professional-type guys that know what they're doing!" And they didn't let any of this affect them, and they tattooed this poor guy, one would take turns. To this day, I mean, those three guys along with Nunley at linebacker, my first game—I couldn't believe how they had it in their mind, these guys weren't going to stop us.

I played in Super Bowls and won Super Bowls but still, this is pretty much the highlight, because of those formative years playing before the biggest crowds ever.

A lot of memories of the Michigan Experience revolved around first games, or last games. The last game at the stadium generated the most emotions back in the early 1950s. Even the hard bitten and "tough as nails" Roger Zatkoff remembers that last trip down the tunnel at the Big House.

> **Roger Zatkoff**: *My final game as a senior was against Purdue. And, you know, we won that game, our final game in the Michigan Stadium and we won that game. And then that was, you know, to me, a kind of a highlight. You know, the realization that this was it, you were never going to be playing in a stadium again. And it was your final game. It was a very special memory, you know, and frankly, I had fun that day. I had a story the referee came to me, and in those days, you could chuck an end as he was coming across the field, okay. And I'm beating up on this guy. So, the referee in the second, third quarter comes to me and said, "Will you ease off?" And I said, "What do you mean, 'ease off?'" He said, "You're killing that kid!" And I said, "Am I doing anything illegal?" He said, "No, but ease off on him, will ya?" But I kept beating up on him as he's coming across, I mean, he wasn't catching anything in my area!*

Quarterback John Wangler also remembers his last game at Michigan Stadium. Interestingly enough, like Roger Zatkoff, it came against Purdue, and it was just as emotional.

> **John Wangler**: *I remember my last game, though, at Michigan Stadium, as you feel the same as a senior going out. I remember on the sidelines how emotional you are going in the tunnel, and the last time you touch the banner, and then warming up. We were playing Purdue and if they won, they were gonna go the Rose Bowl. It was Mark Herrman, and that was his big game. You know, if he had a good game, he probably would have won the Heisman, and they would have gone to the Rose Bowl.*
>
> *I just remember warming up and I was, like, in tears. There was just so much emotion. I was just crying warming up and they—they put a camera, like, right in my face. We were all crying, all the seniors. It was just—it was really, you know, an emotional day, and then we went out, shut Purdue out. It was special.*

As I put this Michigan Experience section together, I tried—through the voices of these Michigan legends—to explain a little bit of why it is so special to all of us who played in maize and blue. There are a lot of nuances from each voice that give a perspective as to what was important to them. They're not all the same, but the final conclusion is clear—it is different at Michigan.

I want you to hear, now, from All-American center Steve Everitt. To say Steve is a bit unconventional is an understatement. He's a free spirit, and you never know what he might say. But when I asked him about his Michigan Experience, he never wavered from a narrative that we've heard time after time.

Steve Everitt: *I mean, everything about being here, like, I mean—I played in the NFL for eight years. And there's not, like, there's not a team I played on, like, after I left Michigan that came even close. I mean, I would have died on the field for this team, you know, and if we could have played for 20 years here, I would have. Like, I was—I was ready to be done with the NFL. You know, I didn't want to go out there and kill myself for that.*

Bo made me cut my hair when I came to school, and that wasn't a big issue. I mean, I didn't grow it out until I left, you know. Moeller, I mean—I got kicked off the team a couple of times for instances that we don't need to get into right now. You know, I had to run with Gittleson on my own at five in the morning for six weeks at a time, a couple times. So that's unconventional, I mean, I think it was all pointed towards, you know, the goal.

I don't know—I mean, there's guys here I haven't seen for 10 years, you know, and it's like you see them for two seconds, and it's like we were just hanging out yesterday. There's just that unbreakable bond that you've bled with these guys. Not that that doesn't happen in other schools, but I don't know, coming from where I came from down in Miami, and I grew up like, you know, a Miami Hurricane fan and a Florida fan, but there's no history with those schools like Michigan. This is just untouchable tradition and to be a part of it, to be mentioned with guys over the years that you idolize, you know—like Jumbo Elliot—and you just throw your name in the ring with those guys, and that right there is enough to justify your existence.

This whole exercise of trying to explain or quantify the idea of a Michigan Experience was a concept head coach Lloyd Carr had been thinking about for years. Coach Carr, who was always looking for ways to get his teams to understand what a privilege it was to play for Michigan, wanted these young men to realize when you played at Michigan, you became part of a tradition, you became part of a brotherhood—a brotherhood that has lasted for years. While he was attempting to teach these new players the history of Michigan football, he wanted them to somehow experience the legends that had played before them, and the legacies these legends had left behind. What better setting for this exercise than Michigan Stadium itself? Well, Lloyd came up with the perfect plan, and he borrowed it from a broadcasting legend.

Lloyd Carr: *Well, I had read an article in the summer of '95, an interview with Keith Jackson. He was talking about what he loved about college football. You know, basically the thing he said he loved most about college football was the tradition. And he said, in the course of this article, you know, "If you— if you really want to know what tradition is," he said, "Some Friday evening, about nine o'clock, go into Michigan Stadium and look around," and he said, "You can feel the spirit, the ghosts of all the great games and all the great players and all the great coaches who have built the tradition at Michigan." And, you know, honestly, I thought that was just an incredible statement. And it really does sum up what a lot of what Michigan is all about.*

And so, I thought, you know, these young players may think I'm crazy, but the Friday night before training camp ended, a week before our first game, before that Virginia game, we had meetings here, and about nine o'clock we broke the meeting. I said, "Okay, men, follow me." So, we walked out over across the railroad tracks and went over to the stadium. In Jackson's statement in this article, he said, "You know, every year, you have a changing of the guard, you have a new group of seniors playing their last game, and you'd have a new group of freshmen coming in." I told the players, I said, "You know, there's a changing of the guard, here. You know, this team has a short lifespan, and it's what you do with it that determines what kind of legacy you leave here."

And then we broke up, and each position coach took his players and told them about some of the games that they had remembered. Then every guy spent some time with himself, and it's been something I've done every year since then. And it has really become a part of our tradition, because these guys get an opportunity, you know—it's amazing now, the freshmen have done it four times. And so, the seniors, when they're going in there for the last time, they have a lot of memories.

EPILOGUE

As we come to the close of the *Voices of Michigan Stadium*, I'm well aware that there's no way I've covered it all. The stadium and the memories created on that hallowed ground are so individual and personal, it's impossible to cover it all for every Michigan fan. Hopefully, we've gone back in history and brought you the first 100 years of Michigan football into some focus.

There are names and voices we missed along the way—maybe some of your favorites didn't get mentioned. And for that, I apologize. There were a couple of things I did want to accomplish, though, and I think we got pretty close. One, I wanted you to experience the feeling of sitting at the dinner table with these Michigan football legends and experiencing their stories. Stories about their triumphs, their failures and their unique memories. I wanted to take you behind the scenes to learn of football exceptionalism in maize and blue. And I think we accomplished that, too.

I wanted to convey the almost mystical and emotional attachment that this great stadium and this great football program at this great university has on the young men that have competed under the Michigan banner. It is unique, it is special, it is unforgettable! I'll close by simply saying, it is all that and more.

Thanks, and Go Blue!

ABOUT THE AUTHOR

Jim Brandstatter is a veteran of 50 years in the sports broadcasting industry and a former football player for the University of Michigan Wolverines. After being honored with All Big Ten recognition as an offensive tackle after his senior season in 1971, Jim began a sports broadcasting career at a TV station in Saginaw, Michigan. From those beginnings came a career that included 43 years on University of Michigan football broadcasts as the play-by-play announcer and color commentator. In addition to being the "Voice of Michigan Football," Jim served 31 years as the color commentator for the Detroit Lions football team on their radio broadcasts. He also hosted the Michigan Football coach's show, *Michigan Replay*, which was later renamed *Inside Michigan Football*, from 1980-2022. His career has garnered numerous honors and awards, including being named a two-time recipient of Michigan's Sportscaster of the Year award and being inducted into the Michigan Sports Hall of Fame. Jim has authored two best-selling books, *Tales from Michigan Stadium* and *Tales from Michigan Stadium--Volume II*. His third authoring venture, *Voices of Michigan Stadium*, is a virtual audio history of Michigan football with some of the greatest names in Wolverine history actually telling their stories through interviews Jim recorded and saved during his years at the heart of the U of M football program.

Jim lives in Michigan with his wife Robbie, who he has been married to since 1980. When not working or finding some project to occupy their time, Jim and Robbie love to travel. They also spend time in northern

Michigan enjoying a cottage they built on the shores of Lake Huron in the mid 1980s. Jim loves to play golf, go fishing, read spy novels, play around with his photography equipment, create slideshows on his computer, and prepare unique recipes from his extensive cook-book collection.

Website: jimbrandstatter.com
Facebook: Jim Brandstatter76
Twitter: @jimbrandstatter
YouTube Channel: The Brandy Show
Podcast: The Brandy Show, Conversations with...